OTHER BOOKS BY PAUL FUSSELL

Theory of Prosody in Eighteenth-Century England
Poetic Meter and Poetic Form
The Rhetorical World of Augustan Humanism:
    Ethics and Imagery from Swift to Burke
Samuel Johnson and the Life of Writing
The Great War and Modern Memory
Abroad: British Literary Traveling Between the Wars
The Boy Scout Handbook and Other Observations
Class: A Guide Through the American Status System
Thank God for the Atom Bomb and Other Essays
Wartime: Understanding and Behavior
    in the Second World War

EDITOR

English Augustan Poetry
The Ordeal of Alfred M. Hale
Siegfried Sassoon's Long Journey
The Norton Book of Travel
The Norton Book of Modern War

CO-EDITOR

Eighteenth-Century English Literature

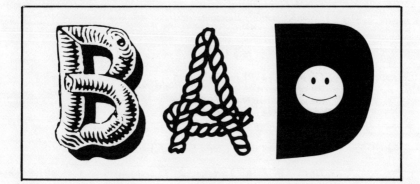

or,
THE DUMBING
OF AMERICA

Paul Fussell

SUMMIT BOOKS
New York • London • Toronto • Sydney • Tokyo • Singapore

SUMMIT BOOKS
Simon & Schuster Building
Rockefeller Center
1230 Avenue of the Americas
New York, New York 10020

10 9 8 7 6 5 4 3 2 1

Library of Congress Cataloging in Publication Data

Fussell, Paul
    Bad or, the dumbing of America / Paul Fussell.
      p.   cm.
    1. United States—Social life and customs—
1971–   2. United States—Popular culture.
I. Title: Dumbing of America.
E169.04.F87   1991
973.92—dc20   91-23587
                                                      CIP
ISBN: 0-671-67652-0

The author wishes to gratefully acknowledge Gary
McMahon for use of the poem "The Two Things in
Life That I Really Love."

ACKNOWLEDGMENTS

For encouragement and various kinds of help, I am indebted to Marcy Behringer, Terry Doherty, Betty Carol Floyd, Tucky Fussell, Samuel Wilson Fussell, Jennifer Herman, F. J. Logan, Jack Lynch, Sheldon Meyer, John Scanlan, James Silberman, and Kristin van Ogtrop. Judith Pascoe and Kay Whittle have been admirable and cheerful research assistants. Don Lessem's *The Worst of Everything*, although focusing on bad instead of BAD, has been indispensable, and so have Richard Boyer and David Savageau's *Places Rated Almanac*, Vince Staten's *Unauthorized America*, and George Toomer's *American Extremes*. And again and always, thanks to my wife, Harriette Behringer, for her company.

To the Memory of
PROFESSOR HAMILTON MARTIN SMYSER,
late of Connecticut College,
fond of remembering a Harvard professor who
often shook his head and muttered,
"Bad, BAD, VERY BAD."

CONTENTS

12   CONTENTS

WHAT IS **BAD** ?

What's the difference between bad and BAD? Bad is something like dog-do on the sidewalk, or a failing grade, or a case of scarlet fever—something no one every said was good. BAD is different. It is something phony, clumsy, witless, untalented, vacant, or boring that many Americans can be persuaded is genuine, graceful, bright, or fascinating. Lawrence Welk is a low example, George Bush a high. For a thing to be really BAD, it must exhibit elements of the pretentious, the overwrought, or the fraudulent. Bathroom faucet handles that cut your fingers are bad. If gold-plated, they are BAD. Dismal food is bad. Dismal food pretentiously served in a restaurant associated with the word *gourmet* is BAD. Being alert to this distinction is a large part of the fun of being alive today, in a moment teeming with raucously overvalued emptiness and trash. Addressing himself on his fiftieth birthday in a poem titled "Ode to Me," Kingsley Amis found it somewhat comforting that more than half his life, at least, had been spent in years before the great contemporary explosion of BAD:

13

> . . . bloody good luck to you, mate,
> That you weren't born too late
> For at least a chance of happiness
> Before unchangeable crappiness
> Spreads all over the land—

and he's talking about England, not yet entirely enthralled
by BAD because of its counterweight of pre-publicity an-
tiquity. The great crappiness is essentially American, for
reasons that will become clear as we go along. But there is
a slight consolation, which Amis points out in *Lucky Jim:*
"The one indispensable answer to an environment bris-
tling with people and things one thought were bad was to
go on finding out new ways in which one could think they
were bad." This book hopes to suggest some new ways.

But it will focus not on BAD alone. It will deal also
with numerous awful things to be met with in the United
States which if not offensive because pretentious, are offensive because banal, stupid, or subadult. One striking
thing about this country above all others is the omnipo-
tence of "presentation." A thing that is palpably bad
doesn't stay bad very long before someone praises it and
thus elevates it to BAD, and soon it is celebrated everywhere as highly desirable. It's as if Americans were so
insecure, so timid about relying on their own decent tastes
and instincts, that they welcome every possible guru to
instruct them about what is good (that is, BAD) and to
encourage them to embrace it. So the things I deal with
that are currently only bad are worth noticing because
they constitute the raw material out of which BAD is finally made.

Plain bad has always been with us. It goes back as far
as the history of artifacts. In Rome there was certainly a
chariot-wheel maker who made bad wheels, a wineseller
who dealt in crappy wine. Introducing sawdust into bread-

stuffs is a time-honored practice, but it becomes BAD only when you insist that the adulterated bread is *better* than any other sort. BAD, that is, is strictly a phenomenon of the age of hype—and, of course, a special will-to-believe in the audience. To achieve real BAD, you have to have the widest possible gap between what is said about a thing and what the thing actually is, as experienced by bright, disinterested, and modest people. There was a bit of BAD visible as far back as 1725 or so, when the earliest newspaper began printing ads, and by the nineteenth century BAD was well developed, especially in America, as various passages in *The Adventures of Huckleberry Finn* attest. In the Duke of Bridgewater's carpetbag are numerous handbills whose office is to transform bad into BAD. For example, "The celebrated Dr. Armand de Montalban, of Paris, will lecture on the Science of Phrenology," while another represents him as the "world-renowned Shakespearean tragedian, Garrick the Younger, of Drury Lane, London." But the Duke and the Dauphin's triumph is their poster for THE ROYAL NONESUCH, to be performed "3 nights only" at the courthouse, LADIES AND CHILDREN NOT ADMITTED. If you're expecting to be purged of pity and fear by a "tragedy" and you are confronted only with an elderly tramp cavorting naked on a stage with his body painted in gaudy colors, you have been present at one of the primary nineteenth-century outcrops of BAD, Overt Swindle Department.

But for genuine deep BAD, you have to arrive at the twentieth century, especially that part of it following the Second World War. The Vietnam War is as good an example as any of the way something bad could be made to seem acceptable for quite a while, until people began to see that what was bad was really BAD, with Lyndon Johnson and William Westmoreland serving as admen. As the music critic Virgil Thomson perceived about symphony and opera, so shrewd and ubiquitous is "paid publicity" that rugged and sometimes contemptuous criticism is, as he says, "the only antidote." But even then, few newspapers rejoice to print scathing notices, for, as Lewis H. Lapham has observed, they are largely engaged in ladling out indiscriminate dollops of optimism and complacency, preserving "the myths that the society deems precious, reassuring their patrons . . . that all is well, that . . . the banks are safe, our generals competent, our presidents interested in the common welfare, our artists capable of masterpieces, our weapons invincible and our democratic institutions the wonder of an admiring world."

BAD, all of it. Thus, underneath, this book is about the publicity enterprise propelling modern life, which seems to make it clear that few today are able independently to estimate the value of anything without prompting from self-interested sources. This means that nothing will thrive unless inflated by hyperbole and gilded with a fine coat of fraud. If in some ways the subject suggests the tragic—all those well-meaning people swindled by their own credulity—looked at another way the topic proposes all the pleasures of farce. BAD projects anew and continuously the classic comic motif, the manipulation of fools by knaves. But sadly, at the moment there's no Ben Jonson around to illuminate it, or even an H. L. Mencken.

BAD ADVERTISING

Advertising is the *sine qua non* of BAD, of course, for BAD depends upon and arises only out of it. To have a fraud, you have to have a large distance between the touted grand appearance and the commonplace actuality, a distance perhaps perceivable by the disillusioned customer after buying the item but never before. The larger the distance, the greater the BAD. In ads for Florida real estate and for "homesites" in the Southwest, the distance is astronomical, as likewise in ads for plastic surgery, weight-loss programs, therapy to raise your self-esteem, and light bulbs guaranteed to last five years. And the distance is greatest, virtually untraversable, when the audience is confronted with words like SALE! or SAVE! or any variant of "33% OFF!"

Some advertising, to be sure, is bad rather than BAD, because so inept that no one would fall for it. Like would-be elegant "invitations" that arrive in the mail announcing the Grand Opening of a new chiropractic or dental office,

17

their hope to be mistaken for "social" rather than commercial gestures signaled by a genteel little "RSVP" down in the corner. Beyond calculation is the amount of disillusion these must occasion among the lonely and the innocent who actually reply, and then dress up and attend, to discover their mistake only after they've arrived. Similar mechanisms are fraudulent "press releases" inviting the hapless recipient to flatter himself or herself into the momentary fantasy of being a privileged "media" person, active behind the scenes. These bogus news stories tout the opening of a new parking lot, store, or spa, as if of world-shaking interest, and bear at the top the titillating words "FOR IMMEDIATE RELEASE." Another form of the hopelessly inept come-on is the radio ad—usually for rugs, men's clothing, or jewelry—delivered by the entirely untalented and un-voice-trained owner of the business, who is also having some trouble with dentures. In the retail world, this is the equivalent of vanity publishing in the authorial, laying out money to appear a person of consequence and interest (see *BAD Books*).

Similarly unpersuasive are the brief radio playlets devised by mediocre ad agencies who conceive of listeners as monumentally stupid:

> [Telephone rings]
> "Mrs. Smith?"
> "Yes."
> "Congratulations! Your request for a $50,000 loan has been approved."
> "Oh, thank you! That's wonderful!"
> [Voice offstage, never heard: "Yes, now you're deeply in debt."]

And of course all the old scams persist, like bait-and-switch, or this "Casting Call" addressed to needy, aspiring young actors and appearing as an expensive ad in the theatrical section of a newspaper indispensable among theater people:

CASTING CALL

Hundreds of well-built, clean-shaven male extras (5′9″–6′2″ only) are required to join the cast of over a thousand in the breathtaking, world-renowned production of *Aida* at Giants Stadium, June 1st and 2nd. NO experience necessary!

All very promising—with the exception of the slight doubt that might enter with BAD words like *breathtaking* and *world renowned*. But imagine getting all excited over this ad ("Mom, I've got a great opportunity at last! Everything's breaking for me now. I'm going to line up early and get a part") and then rereading the tiny, tiny print at the bottom of the ad:

The part of "Extras" is a nonpaying role.

If you've ever read Frank Conroy's *Stop-Time*, you'll remember the great yo-yo swindle, in which a con man takes a whole gang of innocent children, and you'll realize anew why the young no longer put much stock in anything their elders tell them.

That casting call is an example of the way BAD can be achieved by type size. More common is the way it is accomplished by language alone. A trustworthy signal that BAD is approaching is the presence of the modifier *luxurious*, as in *luxurious condominium*. *Luxury* anywhere is a bad sign, but perhaps most notably when associated not with a car but with a *motor car*, where archaism comes to the assistance of pretentiousness. Other words to beware of around auto merchandisers are CELEBRATION! (sometimes

more honestly SELLABRATION!), EVENT!, and any sugges-
tion of *Passing the Savings on to You*. But *luxury* is the most
potent of BAD words, comparable to *gourmet* elsewhere
(see *BAD Restaurants*). Another index of BAD is the presence of *designer*, almost always a warning that the lamb is
about to be fleeced. *Pride of ownership*, likewise, is custom-
arily attendant on something grossly overpriced and aimed
at the most pathetically insecure among us. *Booze* is surely
a low word, and *liquor* a blunt one. Neither is likely to have
the BAD drawing power of *spirits*, suggestive somehow of
an ethereal world as well as a pleasantly snobbish
nineteenth-century one. Experience has shown that words
like *Fine Food and Spirits* seldom fail to suck in the usual
clients of BAD, the pretentious and the illiterate. Like the
word *realty* for land and houses. How bogus British can
you get?

Now and then a practitioner of BAD is forced by public exposure to reveal the true nature of the product. For
years Chrysler has been unloading its troubling surplus
inventories by insisting that its leather upholstery is not
just any old leather, of the sort you might make a volleyball
or lederhosen out of, but "Corinthian Leather." The company finally confessed in the *Wall Street Journal* that the
leather comes not from Corinth but from Newark. The
name was chosen because a reference book suggested that
Corinthian connotes rich desirability, appealing to people
who are, if "dissolute," at least lovers of "luxury, as the
people of Corinth were said to be"—which is why, by the
way, Saint Paul selected them to receive one of his loudest
moral blasts. He told them, "It is reported commonly that
there is fornication among you. . . ." Pressed, the Chrysler
Corporation would have to admit that Corinthian Leather
is just words and never saw Corinth at all.

Other BAD mechanisms for moving goods include
ads that carefully avoid—as if addressing only gentlemen

and ladies well above such considerations—mentioning price. It's sad to report that publishers are now becoming guilty here, joining such traditional offenders as hucksters of costly clothes and jewelry. Again, it used to be an axiom of BAD advertising that to sell anything you had to bring it in proximity to a pretty girl, who might be pictured smiling at an outboard motor or threshing machine. Now, thanks to the years of Reaganism, the girl has been displaced by the flag, especially in notably honky and mercantilist venues like Irvine, California, and Shady Grove, Maryland. Competition in those places has caused flag hypertrophy ("My flag is bigger than your flag"), and now some flags flying above used- ("previously owned") car lots and liquor ("spirits") stores measure a full fifteen by twenty-five feet. On flagpoles a hundred feet tall, they can be seen for miles, proclaiming the unimpeachable Americanism of the BAD displayer.

But speaking of fake patriotism, to experience really deep BAD in action, you have to examine closely the pseudo-patriotic ads published by corporations up to no good. "Public Service" is the phrase invoked to shroud the actuality, "Private Service," and these ads come close to the quintessence of BAD because of the immense and impudent distance between the "Public" appearance and the greedy, private actuality. A lobbying group for the nuclear power industry, which hopes you're too ignorant to know about the industry's record of careless contempt for the health and lives of others, doesn't even have the guts to name itself honestly. It calls itself the "U.S. Council [!] for Energy Awareness" and inserts ads in newspapers arguing that "foreign oil," depicted as a particularly disgusting cobra preparing to strike, is a hazard which can "poison America's economy and our national security." The upshot is that to save our country and safeguard the future of our children, etc., we need more nuclear plants, and we need to get rid of the government regulations which "stifle" the operation of the ones we have, and why don't you people who know about Chernobyl just shut up and let us make our profits? Indeed, the "danger" is not from nuclear plants at all. It's from "importing so much oil."

But an even more egregious example of deep BAD is the patriotism of the cigarette business. One shrewd company has actually engineered an alliance with the National Archives to celebrate the Bill of Rights, and has somehow corralled Lech Walesa into coming out in favor of "Freedom"—implicitly, the freedom to wheedle your less intelligent fellow citizens into enslaving themselves to nicotine addiction. "I'm not sure," Walesa is quoted as saying, "the American people have any idea how blessed they are to have the Bill of Rights."

Light up, America, and inhale deeply, deeply. It's your patriotic duty. That is very BAD advertising, but you can be sure that worse will come.

BAD AIRLINES

The United States is the only highly industrialized country with privately owned airlines, which means that profit-grabbing and the attendant fraud will dominate their operations, inviting them to engage in BAD in a big way. Their hope is that we, their clients, are gravely un-civilized, as ignorant of the distinction between comfort and misery as between food and damp laundry. They hope also that we are devoid of memory, and thus capable, for example, of wiping entirely from our consciousness the inexplicable failure of a Northwest Airlines crew in 1987 to deploy the flaps on takeoff from Detroit, killing 156 trusting people. The industry thrives on public ignorance. It hopes we are historically so uninstructed that we don't know that before the rapid proletarianization of air travel after the Second World War, it used to be almost elegant, or at least pleasant. Of a flight in the 1930s, Paul Bowles remembers, "I had my own cabin with a bed in it, and under sheet and blankets I slept during most of the flight."

Flying four decades later, he couldn't avoid noticing, unequivocally, that "the world had worsened." The result? "I no longer wanted to travel."

The air-travel industry hopes too that we'll forget what fun it used to be to travel on trains and ocean liners and to meet secure, unanxious people and converse with them, a civil distance separating bodies. You could eat real food without abrading your neighbor's elbows, and space and comfort actually favored civilized human intercourse instead of silences or snarls. There's an eloquent bit of dialogue in a Noël Coward play that should be better known:

> "How was your flight?"
> "Well, aeronautically it was a great success. Socially, it left quite a bit to be desired."

Social conditions are probably the worst on planes making the New York–southern Florida run, aboard which New Yorkers heading for vacations are likely to include, as journalist John Arnold reports, "your raving drunks, your drug smugglers, your migrating hookers, your transvestites, your mental patients, your escaped convicts heading south, and a man who thinks he's Elvis Presley," who passes out photographs of himself and grants Elvis autographs. On a train or a liner, you could escape a bore—and the United States breeds more of them than any other country—by the usual social means: pleading an obligation nearby or an almost forgotten social appointment. Now, a total reversal of that scene. With both of you strapped in, every time you risk victimization by your tedious neighbor.

If we are, as is often asserted, living in the Information Era, the airlines are contributing as little as possible to it. Pan Am certainly doesn't want the news to spread very broadly that in a five-year period in the 1980s it was fined over $100,000 by the FAA for violating safety regulations. Nor is it likely itself to publicize the news that during 1988, nineteen FAA agents, testing Pan Am security, smuggled firearms aboard quite undetected. Eastern Airlines probably will not broadcast the news that it has paid in fines over $9 million for violating FAA safety rules, although it could not prevent our knowing that in July 1990, nine of its managers were hit with a sixty-count indictment alleging cover-ups of faulty maintenance in order to make more money. No wonder Eastern went broke and vanished from the BAD scene.

But in every respect the airlines are a leading theater of BAD, and the truth is seldom in them. On one American Airlines flight the voice of the steward was heard to say, "For your convenience, this plane is divided into smoking and nonsmoking sections." Instead of *for your convenience,* read *as required by federal law.* The misrepresentation there is like the whole wide-body publicity fraud. An innocent traveler, reading an ad asserting, "We have the most wide-bodies to Europe," might imagine that wide-bodied aircraft are a boon to the traveler. But just the opposite: on a wide-body you can cram in more seats and intensify discomfort while making more profit. If you tried to put into an average middle-class living room the number of people the airlines shoehorn into a comparable space on a wide-body, you'd have sixty people there. Indeed, it's astonishing the way airlines have almost succeeded in persuading their clients that size is to their benefit. One airline speaks of the "spaciousness" of its 747s, when the least bright of its passengers might perceive in a second that for each passenger there is less space and thus worse service and greater discomfort. But listen to a TWA ad: "We never skimp on air travel comfort. Enjoy full . . . service aboard our spacious, wide-bodied jets." The more *spacious*, the longer the line trying to get into the toilets.

That sort of BAD is an airline specialty, apparent even on the ground, where the ticket agents are apparently trained in dissimulation about delayed departure times and canceled flights to keep you from finding out the horrible truth in time to shift to another airline. In fact, the more you fly, the more the fact will strike you that the airlines are one of the main current sources of fiction. The distance between image and actuality there must occasion more disillusion than most things even in America. Imagine a decent, credulous soul setting out to fly to Europe for the first time, persuaded by BAD air-scam that flying there is chic, comfortable, and convenient. Imagine this naïf encountering the long and ambiguous check-in lines, the long-delayed takeoff with attendant fraudulent alibis, the discovery that the assigned seat is one of nine in a row and much too narrow, and that the tiny space between the rows prevents getting one's legs into any sort of comfortable position. Then imagine what passes through this poor passenger's mind and soul when he realizes, once the obligatory TV is turned on, that he has volunteered to become a captive audience for commercials flogging duty-free goods as well as the notion that the aircraft he's in is a wonder of comfort and style. And that only scratches the surface. (See *BAD Restaurants.*)

God will surely punish one airline for distributing with its meals a little card containing a suggested grace for passengers to say, as if the airline were in the piety business instead of the dissimulation sweepstakes. Better to distribute a prayer for increasingly rigid FAA inspection and for renewed enforcement of laws against deceptive advertising.

BAD AIRPORTS

First bad airports, then BAD. Just as the airlines won't publicize their BAD news, so the International Federation of Airline Pilots Associations doesn't publicize what it knows—about hazardous airports. Los Angeles International, for example, is one of the worst, awarded a "Black Star" by the pilots for its "critical deficiencies." Chief among them is a noise-abatement rule requiring planes landing at night to use a runway badly lighted and usually furnished with a tailwind, a spooky novelty for pilots trained to land, of course, into the wind.

Another horror is Washington, D.C.'s National Airport: runways are too short, and complex last-minute maneuvers are required for arriving planes. "It's a mess," concludes John Galipault of the Aviation Safety Institute, but the airline industry is unlikely to tell you much about it lest you begin agitating for the development of nationalized high-speed rail service, as in Europe. Chicago's Midway Airport is located in the middle of a crowded

residential district. It also features short runways with a re-
markable concrete wall at the end of one of them—a sound
barrier to soothe the nerves of the neighbors, but a constant
menace to any plane arriving with weak brakes. But even
these facilities are safe and easy compared with San Diego's
notorious International Airport, located in the center of
town. The approach enables you to peer into the office windows of the nearby tall buildings. Short runways, too.

The problem with San Francisco International is different. There you have parallel runways too close together,
on which pilots are urged, to reduce air-traffic congestion
and to maximize profits for everyone, to land simulta-
neously, "wingtip to wingtip," as Michael Walker notes in
Spy magazine, inviting death by sheer fright. Yet, declares
Walker, you are not supposed to know about these things:
"The relative plane-worthiness of our airports is information not routinely shared with the public"—and this in the
Information Age.

That's the bad. The BAD, on the other hand, is routinely promulgated to convey the impression that the
airports are unimprovable, rational, comfortable, and up-
to-date. In *The Air Traveler's Handbook: The Complete Guide
to Air Travel, Airplanes, and Airports* (1989), we are vouchsafed a schematic drawing purporting to represent the
"Anatomy of an Air Terminal." This proves so ideal, if not
idyllic, that it bears no resemblance to any airport experienced by actual people. In this one, for example, there's a
medical center where you can get necessary vaccinations.
In addition, the reader is assured, "large airports may have
operating rooms." The restaurants "are often open all
night to the general public." Travel bureaus are there, it is
said. (I've never seen a single one at an American airport:
they would be nice to run to when you learn that your
flight to Cleveland has been canceled and you're trying to
find out if it's possible to get there from here.) This pic-

tured ideal airport has automatic doors and escalators which work, and it offers also "showers and baths." The airport in Copenhagen does, but not those in the United States.

Here, what we are offered is not just an absence of those amenities, but also few places to sit down; lots of ghastly canned music; an absence of clocks to inform those (the Information Age again) arriving from a different time zone what time it is; incomprehensible public-address announcements, some of which one suspects are important; rows of vandalized telephones, sometimes with urine on the floor of the booths; only the bad local newspapers on sale, as if those arriving from a distance are as stupid as the locals; security people operating the X-ray scanners who giggle and socialize; booths labeled "Foreign Money Exchange," which prove, after you've worked your way up to the window (twenty minutes for that), to sell and buy no zlotys, dinars, or Turkish pounds, and hardly to have heard of them.

One specialty of really BAD airports is ineptly arranged departure facilities, so that the farther you move in "the boarding process," the more necessary facilities are withdrawn without warning. As you proceed, with return forbidden, you leave behind banks, newsstands, bars, and toilets, so that you are finally left waiting for an hour or so (suddenly discovered "mechanical problems" with the aircraft) cold sober, your pocket full of unwanted strange currency, with nothing to read and nowhere to urinate. You are confined in the "boarding lounge," which is as little like a lounge as conceivable. Infants are crying, standees are shifting from foot to foot, and bores are already preparing their repertoires.

And the *Air Traveler's Handbook* actually titles one of its sections "Traveling for Pleasure." There may be some clue to the reason for this and similar incursions of BAD in the

Acknowledgments in that book where you'll find heartfelt thanks conveyed to Boeing Commercial Airplane Co., Avis Rent A Car, Thomas Cook & Son, Ltd., Grumman American Aviation Corp., Pan Am, TWA, and the Port Authority of New York and New Jersey.

This last is responsible for what is probably the very worst airport in the United States, John F. Kennedy International, a monument to the mess occasioned by unregulated free enterprise, with its separate buildings for different airlines and its lack of a clear, uniform system of information. Dorothy Storck, a journalist flying from New York to Vienna and planning to write on her laptop computer on the way, was informed just before boarding that she couldn't take the laptop aboard, lest it explode. Finding no checkroom or storage lockers (they'd been removed years ago to prevent the insane from lodging bombs in them), she was obliged "in desperation" to phone a friend to come to the airport to take away her computer. From this experience and many others, Storck has concluded that JFK is "the most user-unfriendly airport in the world." No surprise, really, that there was no place to store her laptop. "Since [JFK] has no use for such exotica as a decent dining room, you could hardly expect a safe storage space," she says.

And it's all concealed by BAD—by the smiles of the waitresses, aka flight attendants; the classy quasi-naval uniforms of the cockpit crew; the theme songs and slogans; the mileage "clubs" that are not clubs; the acute inconvenience and discomfort passing for up-to-date and "luxurious"; and the implication that this is all an improvement on those old trains and ships. So sit back and enjoy your flight.

There's no alternative.

BAD ARCHITECTURE

There's plenty of bad architecture around, featuring stairways that take you up to blank walls; embarrassing shapeless and nameless spaces, neither rooms nor corridors, whose human purpose is unknown; seven-foot ceilings inviting you to shuffle along stooped over; "balconies" where no one could stand or sit; and street entrances without a portico or rooflet, so that you must get wet when you leave in the rain.

But those things are not the topic here. We are concerned with BAD—architecture so ludicrously and expensively pretentious as to become ridiculous when occupied by mere second-rate human beings like us. BAD buildings are those that huff and puff and brag—and come out looking like shoeboxes. Or like the candy box that is the Kennedy Center for the Performing Arts in Washington, D.C. Its pomposity and would-be grandeur suggest it as a site for nothing less than a nonstop presentation of *Aïda* with immense heroic processions and herds of real ele-

31

phants and camels, with everyone speaking—nay, singing—the best possible Italian. But actually, this grandiose and repellent structure houses only minor road shows passing through, stupid Broadway comedies, failing musicals, and low pop entertainments. Its grandiloquent 600-foot-long lobby corridor resembles nothing so much as the pompous "gallery" in Hitler's Chancellery, and indeed Ada Louise Huxtable has found it hard to think of this whole building without being reminded of the taste of Hitler and his sycophantic architect, the late war criminal Albert Speer.

Perhaps Norman Mailer wasn't just vaporing when he used the word *totalitarian* to stigmatize the main tendencies in contemporary architecture. Indeed, the central campus of the State University of New York at Stony Brook looks— like many other such—precisely as if the Germans had won the war and were now installed here, imposing National Socialist taste everywhere. And the most accurate terms for the charmless, merely tall and huge blunt buildings of the World Trade Center in New York are Hitler-resonant as well: *brutal* and *despotic*. Dull and witless, expressive only of dumb raw power, they are widely touted as among the major achievements of the late twentieth century.

But architectural gigantism on the East Coast can't compare with its Southwestern manifestation, say in Las Vegas, where you can view exemplary BAD in the clumsy, outsized whorehouses and other hotels of the Strip. A new one, the so-called Excalibur, is now, with 4,032 rooms, the biggest hotel in the world, overtaking the Rossiya in Moscow, with 3,150 rooms, which used to be the biggest, and one of the worst. At the Excalibur, the telephone operators sign off with "Have a Royal Day." (See *BAD Hotels.*) The center of the Excalibur, where clients enter, is a gigantic gaudy rendering of "King Arthur's Castle," with spires and turrets, moat and drawbridge, and similar Disneyisms. Inside, where customers are addressed as lords and ladies, the experience of vulgar excess is like contemplating the interior of the Metropolitan Opera House at Lincoln Center, New York, whose overdone scarlet and gilt, tassels and swags, impress the same people excited by the phrase *Designer Towels:* tacky would-be grandeur, attended, backstage, by the latest extravagant technology, turntables, elevators, computerized stage lighting. Overproduction as usual, but little taste, and thus a conspicuous incarnation of BAD. Like the whole of Lincoln Center, "a foolish pomposity," in the words of architect Robert Campbell.

Back in 1720, Jonathan Swift exhorted a young clergyman to preach unpretentiously, avoiding the temptation to impress his listeners with metaphysical terms and similar university flourishes. A public speaker, Swift insisted, should aim at "that simplicity without which no human performance can arrive to any great perfection." Architecture, the most visible and unignorable human performance, is the place where people most publicly derive their understanding of themselves, and contemporary Americans have great trouble achieving that frank, unshowy Swiftian simplicity. Consider the façade of the American Embassy in London. Not content with a simple horizontal expanse, dull but not nasty, some bright improver thought to appliqué on it an immense banal gilt eagle, so that everyone would Get It. It's like the ruin of the Vietnam Memorial in Washington, once a triumph of throat-catching understatement and simplicity, until a group of literalists, enacting precisely the dynamics of the Dumbing of America, had to erect "lifelike" sculptures nearby. (See *BAD Public Sculpture.*)

Straight lines, inevitable in the steel, aluminum, and glass boxes which now pass for buildings, are death to the imagination. As Renaissance architects and builders knew, curves and rounded surfaces are indispensable to the human desire to think of oneself as subtle, varied, valuable, and interesting. Equality is one of the ideas glorified by the new architecture, and that might be a good thing, but this equality is the equality of ignorance, a celebration of the assumption that no one has sufficient experience or learning to enjoy the allusive exercise required by traditional architectural details like balustrades, crockets, finials, metopes, or triglyphs. The current architecture implicitly patronizes its users and audiences. An escalator going up only one flight assumes that the stairway is obsolete. The escalator alludes to nothing while the stairway it replaces at least alluded to the Spanish Steps, the Santa Scala, Bernini's Scala Regla at the Vatican, and Garnier's Paris Opéra staircase. Many of them, notably, employ the curves desired by the imagination but impossible for the escalator to imitate. Curved moldings, which in interiors used to break up right angles, have gone too, just the way the hardwood door, with paneled moldings and interesting hinges and handles and knobs, has been replaced by the light, cheap flush door, which alludes to nothing. Laid flat and supported at the corners, the flush door becomes the desk without allusion, a fit piece of furniture for the simpleminded buildings it occupies.

In the United States, BAD architecture is rampant because money and profit take clear priority over taste and amenity. But BAD is rampant here too because of the paucity of architectural criticism. Britain has at least Prince Charles to bitch about architectural ugliness and vandalism and tedium. We have no such public figure commenting on architecture, and except for Huxtable and Tom Wolfe, we have hardly any critics who are not the captives of corporate money or university taste. Our need is for many more stigmatizers of BAD. We need, to put it simply, a John Simon of architectural criticism. (And see *BAD Engineering*.)

BAD BANKS

Now that they have exchanged their dignity for publicity and taken to blatant mendacious advertising like everyone else, all banks are, in varying degrees, BAD. Few are capable of resisting the profitable near-deceptive practice of suggesting, on MasterCard bills, that only a portion of the amount due need be paid, the bank likes you so much. The credulous and those not rigorously trained in close reading of difficult texts are thus suckered into a massive 18 percent interest charge unawares.

BAD banks like to treat their clients like proles, enlisted men, or animals, obliging them to enter a roped-off space labeled ENTER HERE, which twists and turns until the head of the queue finally arrives at the tellers' windows. BAD banks never know who you are, even if you've had your money in them for fifty years, and insult you by laboriously checking your signature against a blown-up negative microfiche each time. Banks used to look like marble temples, or even like the grander sort of Episcopal

churches. Now they look like lower-middle-class motel of-
fices with mock-friendly housewives in charge, who still
don't have a clue who you are. The best BAD banks make
you listen to Handel or Mozart; the worst, to selections
from *Stop the World, I Want to Get Off!* or *How to Succeed in
Business Without Really Trying.* BAD banks never deal in
foreign currency and resist engaging in any transaction,
foreign or domestic, which is slightly out of the ordinary.
(And see *BAD Music.*)

BAD BEHAVIOR

To be distinguished, as always, from mere harmless bad, like saying "Have a nice day" to perfect strangers or naming girls Kimberley. When bad behavior becomes aggressive, pretentious, disingenuous, or morally monstrous, it mutates into BAD, something awful which many regard as either morally neutral or quite fine. Example: attending a "networking" "party," where the greedy young exchange business cards in the hope of rising in the commercial world. There, the normal social motive, the quest for friendship or the alleviation of loneliness, is travestied, emerging as simple ambitiousness, and the insensitive "partygoers" imagine that they are engaging in admirable behavior. That sort of simulated or fraudulent, and certainly unearned, friendship or intimacy requires confirmed practitioners of BAD to call strangers by their first names unasked and to jump instantly into the midst of others' private business. Philip Roth has caught the tone exactly, in *Zuckerman Unbound*, in the behavior of Alvin

Pepler, the pest of Nathan Zuckerman, the newly successful novelist. On a New York bus, Pepler suddenly addresses him: "What the hell are you doing on a bus, with
your dough?"

That is an offensive manifestation of BAD, but there
are pathetic ones too. Some retail clerks obliged to work on
commission send their customers little pseudo-friendly,
would-be-genteel printed cards, like this:

> This is just a note to let you know that I was very
> pleased to be able to serve you at _____ . I
> hope that your recent purchase is giving you much
> pleasure and that I will have the opportunity to serve
> you again soon. Please don't hesitate to call me.

Clearly a cry of desperation BADly disguised as an expression of friendly concern.

Miss Manners is an acute spotter of BAD, one of the
most trustworthy current authorities:

> Dear Miss Manners: Many wedding invitations I have
> received have included a small card with the name of
> the store at which the bride is registered. Is this in
> good taste?
>
> Gentle Reader: No. It is in appalling taste. We don't
> require brides nowadays to pretend a lot of things they
> used to pretend, but the pretense that they will be
> surprised and delighted if people want to offer them
> presents is still essential.

Weddings, indeed, offer maximum opportunities for
BAD behavior, like displaying the presents at the recep-
tion, with cards soliciting awe and admiration for each
identified donor, or proceeding without restraint in other
mercantile, mock-"luxurious" directions. Consider the

overflow of BAD in the "Wedding Package" offered by one limousine service ($165 for the first three hours, $30 each additional hour, "Plus 15% gratuity"):

Luxury Chauffeured Limousine [white and stretch, you may be sure]
Professional Driver Dressed in Tuxedo [!]
Red Carpet Runner (from back door of limo to the first step of the ceremony)
Chilled Bottle of Champagne

And for $85 more you can lay on a mock-spontaneous "Balloon Release" of one hundred balloons ("$1 each additional balloon"). Then, to abdicate from all spontaneity, you can order a ready-made JUST MARRIED sign for the back of the limo ($25 extra). That may seem high for a mere mass-produced sign, but for the $25 you also get "Two color streamers on the side of the car," together with "Two color Pom Poms on side of car, Three wedding bells on the front of car, and Four Balloons across rear of car." *That* will make people pay attention to you! One oversight: the company has neglected to think of renting out three to five tin cans to be dragged on strings behind the nuptial vehicle ($10 extra).

The post-Reagan atmosphere of open greed disguised as a good thing has made even high school commencements occasions of unashamed acquisitiveness and duplicity. Currently, you're likely to receive in the spring what looks like an invitation to a social event. Upon close examination, it proves to be an invitation, all right, but an invitation from some seventeen-year-old virtual stranger to send a gift—of money, of course, since you don't know the creature at all. The document is not really an invitation, but an "announcement" with a card bearing the name of the hopeful recipient of your largess, and often an address to which gifts are to be sent.

The telephone has opened up numerous occasions for BAD behavior, like calls beginning "You don't know me, but . . ." And how about programming office phones to make them do cute or rude things, like asking callers to "touch" (not "press") a number on their touch-tone phone (the possibility that they might be so out of it as to own, still, a dial phone would be unthinkable) to get what they want ("To reach our billing department touch three)? (Formerly, before BAD became endemic, the switchboard operator simply connected you.) Another currently stylish form of BAD is asking you to wait ("hold" is the euphemism) while terrible music is played at you (see *BAD Music*). But for real offensiveness, it can't match someone speaking (or pretending to speak) into a "cellular" phone in a car, in the hope of being admired and envied by someone even more vulgar.

Other sorts of BAD behavior are best listed alphabetically:

Alcohol, removing it from alcoholic drinks, thus seeking to have it both ways. *Lite* potations, the result, are very American and very BAD. One should either drink or not drink, but not mess up the pleasure attaching to one indulgence (drinking) by mixing it with the pleasure attaching to another (self-righteousness).

Artificial fibers, putting them where they have no business, in sheets and pillowcases, towels, and napkins especially.

Beeper, wearing one to a party. The person doing this is (to use Woody Allen's rude term) a connectivity asshole. Beepers, both real and counterfeit, are now a common way for insignificant people to imply their high professional and social value. Often met with at networking parties.

Beneficence, congratulating oneself on one's own. For example, including in a wedding invitation a card reading,

We are aware of the plight of the less fortunate and homeless. Please bring a spare article of winter clothing.

The second sentence: acceptable behavior. The first: BAD.

Camcorder, using one to obtrude one's presence at public events, assuming a special right to obstruct and disturb other people, all because one has bought a costly object.

Caps and gowns, dolling up kindergarten children in white crepe-paper ones for their "graduation." Only slightly less BAD is costuming high school graduates in light blue rayon numbers. (And see Addendum to *BAD Colleges and Universities.*)

Cats and dogs, giving them pretentious names to show off your costly education—calling cats Clytemnestra or Hester (after Prynne), dogs Ahab or Toby Belch. The same BAD people likely to do this are those who impose embarrassing names on helpless children, augmenting the number of girls named Eliot or Charles, the number of boys named Dunstan, McGeorge, or Stringfellow.

Celebrities, going all to pieces in the presence of. The very idea of "celebrities" is BAD. Let's have Madonna to dinner!

Driving, inept. In a recent political furor over high auto-accident insurance rates in New Jersey, no one suggested bringing the rates down by simply driving better.

Exercising publicly and conspicuously. This is self-congratulatory and thus BAD behavior at its worst. When this fad began some thirty years ago and spread throughout the middle class, one hoped to stamp it out by spreading the rumor that only sex perverts went in for it. That was doubtless true in part, but

soon hordes of normally decent people began showing off this way, and now the practice of running and
puffing and carrying showy little weights, often with
earphones clapped onto one's head, has gone too far
to be stopped by anything but modesty and good
sense.

Faux-friendly style, the, like retail clerks and waiters asking,
"How are you today?" (See *BAD Restaurants.*)

Hands, clapping them promiscuously on the set of TV shows
like *Wheel of Fortune* or *Family Feud.* This is supposed
to suggest spontaneous enthusiasm and happiness,
but only the naïve will be deceived. What it conveys is
a positive delight in obeying the commands of a cynical TV producer.

Life-style, using the term at all and being always conscious of
one's L. Especially BAD is changing it frequently as
ordered by slick magazines.

Lines (that is, queues), crashing them. Bold line-crashers are
usually people of the lower social orders, accustomed
to fighting for what they get. Their behavior, if understandable, is bad. But BAD is line-crashing by the
more cowardly but no less pushy and greedy middle
and upper-middle classes, who go more subtly to
work. Instead of just intruding themselves in the middle of the line and daring you to do something about
it, they sneak: they insinuate themselves *not in front of
you but at your side.* Counting on your tolerance of am-
biguity, they hope you are willing to ignore the clear
distinction, treasured in the military, between a rank
and a file. They are best dealt with by a sudden, violent, loud, and if possible profane and obscene tirade,
which they have assumed you are too much the gentleman or lady to unleash. The suddenness is what
makes it work.

Military maneuvers, screwing up excessively clever, like the attempt by the Carter administration in April 1980 to rescue the Iranian hostages with helicopters landing in the desert near Tehran. Relying on pretentious equipment (BAD in one of its commonest forms), the attempt failed dismally: once more the United States was disgraced, eight people were killed, five were wounded, and the hostages were not freed. Americans were so humiliated that they went and elected Ronald Reagan. The point: showy technology can't redeem such human constants as stupidity and ineptitude. (And see *BAD Naval Missile Firing.*)

Movies, "colorizing" black-and-white ones. This is an affront against the past; against the convention of black and white, which makes possible all those white ties and tails and white boudoirs and white nightclubs; and against the whole sophisticated idea of artistic convention. As movie critic Leslie Halliwell has said, color in movies is BAD and irrelevant because it "apes reality. . . . Black and white conjure[s] up its own mood and its own comment." Do you want lifelikeness or art? (And see *BAD Newspapers* and *BAD Public Sculpture.*)

Music, talking about it instead of playing it, BAD behavior registering the sense that "cultural" experience must be improving and educational, a curse of ill-educated and insecure but pretentious societies like ours.

Sean, spelling it either Shaun or Shawn, or sometimes even Shawon. It's bad enough to fasten a vividly Irish name onto a boy who has never heard of County Mayo, but to betray by a gauche spelling that you don't know how to pronounce it is BAD, the equivalent of pronouncing Sean Connery's first name *Seen.*

Signs, homemade, displaying at televised sports events. If they say only "Way to Go, Lefty!" they are harmless. If they

say "Fuck the Rangers!" they are bad. But BAD ones
say either

> JOHN 3:16

or

> JOHN 14:6

Whichever, a BAD manifestation of aggressive self-
righteousness.

Speaking in public, running over one's allotted time when. Incompetent and selfish, as well as boring, and a bit of
BAD behavior that gains adherents daily.

Title, awarding oneself an impressive, like Prophet, Reverend,
or Maharishi, or designating oneself a Therapist. (See
BAD Beliefs.)

Traveler's checks, scaring people into buying your brand by implying that if they don't their vacations will be utterly
ruined.

BAD BELIEFS

Every day Americans are exhorted to exercise, jog, de-fat themselves, and generally to pay lots of attention to their bodies. But it's not the American body, gross as it may be, that is the current scandal. It's the American mind. One could say of most Americans what *My Fair Lady*'s Henry Higgins asks about women who pay too much attention to the way their hair looks: "Why don't they straighten up the mess that's *inside?*"

What makes Americans more credulous than other people? Is it the collapse of the educational system, which makes acute reasoning about cause and effect a rarity, and an "elitist" one at that? Is it that more and more Americans have attended *BAD Colleges and Universities* (q.v.)? Or is the current gullibility a compensation for the inevitable disappointments engendered by the common view that life promises everyone splendid rewards, especially the "happiness" the Declaration sets forth as a target? When you find that after all your dogged consumption in obedience to advertising you're still not "happy" ("Is *this* all?"), what to do but seek another dimension of hope by means of auras, Karmic Analysis, Miracle Prayer Cloths, Chakra Balance, crystals, soothsayers, horoscopes, copper bracelets (for that pesky arthritis), UFO abduction, the visit of extraterrestrials ("aliens"), past-life therapy, and out-of-body travel? "Something of a psychiatrical clinic" is the way Thorstein Veblen described this country, and he regarded the whole place as "a case":

> The case of America is . . . not to be fairly understood without making due allowance for a certain prevalent unbalance and derangement of mentality. . . . Perhaps the commonest and plainest evidence of this unbalanced mentality is to be seen in a certain fearsome and feverish credulity with which a large proportion of the Americans are affected.

The American conviction that actuality imposes cruel, and really unfair, limits upon desire leads naturally to the ambition to

TRAVEL OUT OF YOUR BODY

Finally! You can learn to safely and easily leave your physical body—at will—to travel to distant lands, visit family, meet absent lovers, even communicate with spirit beings.
>   —ad, one of thousands in *Fate Magazine*

And the American veneration of practicality can be accommodated by a useful kit providing all you need to escape to Astral Worlds: "*Gateway to the Astral Worlds:* a practical guide to astral projection. Includes book, tape, meditation card, crystal, fragrant oil, and instruction booklet."

It's a sobering thought that people able by law to vote,

serve on juries, own and discharge firearms, drive auto-
mobiles, and walk around freely believe in

Atlantis

The prophecies of Nostradamus ("The instant United
States troops were deployed in the Middle East, I
sold out of my stock of Nostradamus books."—
bookshop employee)

Palmistry

Divination by tarot cards

"Readings" accomplished by crystal gazers, "gifted
seeresses," etc.

The power of pentagrams and similar talismans to
make sure that you will "Win Whenever Gambling"

The power of cardboard pyramids to put an edge on
used razor blades

The roulette wheel's memory and disinclination to repeat itself (or inclination *to* repeat itself)

Creation Science

Preexistence, which proves to be a belief always with
snobbish overtones. As the writer George Toomer
has noted, people conscious of having lived at least
once before were always something grand, never
sewer employees, garbagemen, or shovelers of
dung in the stables of the prerevolutionary French
court.

UFOs, best seen (this is widely believed) on Wednes-
days between 1:00 and 3:00 A.M.

Lucky numbers

The Loch Ness monster

Bigfoot

A room spray compounded of frankincense and
myrrh, whose effect is to "bless" premises sprayed
with it

These beliefs are worse than bad. They are BAD because
they represent an overweening urge to impose one's little

wishes upon a solid, unyielding actuality. But if such beliefs are BAD, worse are the "New Age" con men and
women who take millions annually from their gullible New
Age patsies. To assist them, they devise preposterous,
pompous titles for themselves. One is a Psychometrist, another a Metaphysical Parapsychologist, another a Psycho-
numerologist, another (actually a sub-commonplace
woman) an Ecofeminist, another a Gifted Witch, still another a Nature Priestess. One has designated himself an
"Internationally Acclaimed flutist/composer/healer." One
founded her very own Church of Ageless Wisdom and
appointed herself "Primate Archbishop." (See *BAD Behavior.*) Many are content to be simply Psychics. Contemplating them, the irreverent critic George Toomer can't help
wondering why, if they have access to the secret of life and
other things, they can't use it to "clear up pimples." How
seldom their skill at foretelling allows them to make a killing on the commodities exchange, which would allow them
to flee to the Riviera from the horrible places where they
now live—Skokie, Illinois; Sappington, Missouri; Orlando,
Florida; Emmaus, Pennsylvania; New Bern, North Carolina. One sad sack and pauper, rusticated to Holiday, Florida, knows "How to Precipitate Money" and will tell you
for $8.85, plus $1.50 for postage and handling. And note
the leakage of fatuous self-satisfaction from every pore of
this classified ad from a psychic newsletter, inserted by a
fifty-year-old loser in Utah:

> Am not a serious student, but have varied interests:
> wholistic wellness, dolphin consciousness, karma, past-
> life explorations, crystals, pyramids, ESP, spiritual
> growth, E.T.s, UFOs, channeling, reincarnation, . . .
> psychic awareness, spiritual healing. . . .

"Not a serious student"! "Varied interests"! There you
have the whole bag, the pseudo-scholarly tone affected by

the intellectually deprived. This poor fellow must be the most egregious dupe in the whole state of Utah, a place famous for its ninnies, of the United States the veritable Paphlagonia. (David Hume, "Of Miracles," 1748: "It was a wise policy in that false prophet Alexander [a religious mountebank of the second century] . . . to lay the first scene of his impostures in [the backward Roman province] of Paphlagonia, where . . . the people were extremely ignorant and stupid, and ready to swallow even the grossest delusion.")

Of all these follies, astrology is probably the most popular, and even some civilized people have been known to fall for it. Unhappy with the vulgar materialism of modern life—and who is not?—even Carl Jung reached for a bit of astrology in his search for meaning. Many more Americans than you might imagine believe in astrology, at least in part, and one reason Nancy Reagan's reliance on it in advising the President didn't, like Watergate, bring down the administration is that a great many voters see nothing silly in acting on astrological guidance. Astrologers themselves are beginning to put on professional airs, and the American Federation of Astrologers, to which the best ones belong, regards it as "unethical" to cast a horoscope fraudulently—that is, in the absence of precise information about not just the time of birth but the *place*. A sad fact is that the appeal of astrology now cuts across the classes (see *BAD Colleges and Universities*). A Macy's ad in a newspaper read by New York's most skeptical people offers

WINTUITION,

The Astrological Lucky Numbers Computer, designed by the celebrated astrologer/psychic, Irene Hughes, and Data Base Marketing, Inc. Enter your birth date and today's date and this electronic, hand-held seer displays set after set of your luckiest number combinations. An excellent reference for daily pick 3, daily

pick 4 and weekly lotto as well as for all paramutual
betting circumstances.

Well down below the audience for that, the depths of gullibility extend, until we reach

PETS ARE PSYCHIC TOO!

Send birth date, picture, sex of your
pet for reading. $25.00

That the inability to think which is propelling that sort
of thing is not just American but North American is suggested by a testimonial sent the astrologer who admits
helping Ronald and Nancy Reagan conduct the Republic.
L.J. of Edmonton, Alberta, Canada, writes: "You said I
was going to meet a man. And I met a gentleman on the
bus last week." Q.E.D.

To people like that, convictions of conspiracy come
easily. To them, a matter of crucial importance and a national scandal is the way the government is covering up the
numerous visits of aliens from other worlds. They like to
land in the American Southwest—never near Cal Tech,
Stanford, MIT, or the National Academy of Science. One
famous "manned" UFO containing "16 small human-like
bodies" came to earth near Aztec, New Mexico (no surprise there), and the "ranking military and scientists involved" have conspired to impose a TOP SECRET label on
this event—although it is widely known among residents
of the American Paphlagonia. For $21.95 postpaid you
can acquire a 612-page book revealing the whole business.
Thus, the main enemy of self-realization, transcendence,
and knowledge of the aliens who come here from other

worlds is the United States government. Quite predictable, considering the way it has programmatically "excluded God from the American classroom"—Ronald Reagan. But "science" is also blamable for its pigheaded refusal to learn. Professor James Gleick of Princeton testifies to the cascade of letters he receives from people annoyed that his scientific writings fail to take into account their unassisted discoveries of "new cosmologies . . . mathematical proofs, stock-market strategies, and grand theories of everything." No wonder he says, "Uh Oh, Here Comes the Mailman." Some samples:

> I've notified two universities. . . . I have received *no* response. [My discovery] clears up the confusion in quantum physics.

> This is a letter proposing a new model of the world . . . a duoverse.

> Exobiological intelligence. . . . Great stuff! Pure logic.

> A chemical-biological equation which . . . outlines or explains the difference between a very well designed universe and the universe as it exists today.

> Like the fat lady who shatters the glass with her voice, humanity shall shatter our solar system with fornication.

> I've sent these [ideas] to priests, ministers, schools, newspapers, but nary a peep from any or they just don't give a "hoot."

> Who am I? Suffice it to say for now that I am a Nature Philosopher in the mold of the 17th and 18th centuries. A philosophic generalist is what I call myself.

"What's going on here?" asks Professor Gleick. "We're supposed to be living in an era of sophistication about science, an era of universal education, of public-television science specials, of daily newspaper science pages. Every other high school student seems to have his own computer." Yes, but he has overlooked the immense weight of BAD, the widespread current inability to bring evidence and skepticism to the idea of causality. (See *BAD Colleges and Universities.*)

Serious scientists have tried without notable success to engage openly some of these BAD fantasists and neurotics. A group of zoologists has formed the International Society of Cryptozoology (headquartered in Tucson, Arizona, not the most promising sign) to examine reports of outré creatures like yetis, bigfeet, and Loch Ness monsters. Skepticism and a demand for evidence are supposed to be the guides of this group. But some people, like Professor George Gaylord Simpson, said by Malcolm W. Browne to have been "the dean of American paleontologists," have thought the cryptozoologists just as deeply hoodwinked by their own loose imagery as the true believers. Looking over the whole scene of self-deception and the lust for wonders, Simpson concluded: "Humans are the most inventive, deceptive, and gullible of all animals." Quite so. We are the only mammals who like to make things up and deceive for the pleasure of it—a way of saying that fiction, art, and religion are uniquely human contrivances.

But to believe that God hears and sometimes answers prayers or that after death you're going to be reunited with your parents or that good luck will follow skipping every sidewalk crack or that The Stars Know—these beliefs are not so bad. They become BAD only when, like the Reagans, you let them influence the national affairs of the rest of us, and they become especially BAD when you peddle them to the weak of mind or when you get all sincere and pretentious and full of self-importance and proselytize to convey your unique wisdom to an inattentive world. ("A philosophic generalist is what I call myself.") And when you do that to make money, you are so BAD that you may go to Hell, a place where fires burn everlastingly to torment awful people like you (see Matthew 25:41).

BAD BOOKS

Too big a subject, to be sure, to be dealt with in this limited space. Still, with tens of thousands of books pouring out annually, it is to be expected that not more than a minuscule number can be any good. George Orwell perceived the embarrassing truth:

> It is almost impossible to mention books in bulk without grossly overpraising the great majority of them. Until one has some kind of professional relationship with books one does not discover how bad the majority are.

Not to mention how BAD the majority are.

A way to save time and money is to spot these BAD books before they are published—and even before they are written. A useful hint is to beware of people who talk about the book they're going to write, or the book they say they are writing. Ten to one it will be bad or BAD, for good books are produced by people who prefer writing them to talking about them. The difference is between writing and acting—in the stage sense. The difference is between the lonely private operation and the happy public one, or in extreme cases, between doing something good and showing off. José Ortega y Gasset once wrote, "When I hear a friend, particularly if he is a young writer, calmly announce that he is working on a novel, I am appalled." Why? Because the chances against any novel sticking in the memory or staying on the bookshop shelves longer than eight weeks are astronomical. If you want to be remembered as a clever person and even as a benefactor of humanity, don't write a novel, or even talk about it: instead, compile tables of compound interest, assemble weather data running back seventy-five years, or develop in tabular form improved actuarial information. All more useful than anything "creative" most people could come up with, and less likely to subject the author to neglect, if not ridicule and contempt. In addition, it will be found that most people who seek attention and regard by announcing that they're writing a novel are actually so devoid of narrative talent that they can't hold the attention of a dinner table for thirty seconds, even with a dirty joke.

Another way to spot BAD books before they appear is suggested by a recent news photograph of a young woman writing her book (a novel, one suspects) in a beauty parlor on a laptop word processor, while her hairdresser arranges her ringlets. If this isn't enough, there's a further warning in what she says: "I'm doing a book about the ten years I spent in Asia studying meditation. I do a lot of writing at the salon and fax my publisher in New York from there." *Salon?* Practically *prima facie* evidence of the BADness of her projected book.

Titles, once the book actually gets published—that most of them do not is one of the few consolations of contemporary life—are another handy warning sign. *How You Can Guarantee Success,* by Jim Bakker (I'm not making this up), is a case in point. How about *Healing the Wounds: The Promise of Ecofeminism,* said to contain "essays, stories, poetry, and invocations [!] " uniting the "visions" of both feminism and ecology, "two of the most potent healing visions of our time." You should look out for any book with *Healing* in the title: thus *Love, Peace, and Healing* sends up great dense smoke clouds of warning. Other titles demand flip answers, like *Who's Calling the Shots? How to Respond Effectively to Children's Fascination with War Play and War Toys.* (Answer: recommend that they join the Marine Corps.)

Book ads are the place to look for warnings. It would probably be just as well not to get too excited over a book issued from a post office box in Vermont offering stories told with "consummit skill." Or another, obtainable from a PO box in Georgia, whose ad begins

FIRST TIME OFFER

and continues,

> "A car is a Very Small Room," or how to have successful, happy family automobile travel. Author is an experienced traveler.
> Order now!

Leap to it, world! Or if that seems too earthbound, send for *On Proof for the Existence of God, and Other Reflective Inquiries,* with eighty-five diagrams, from a PO box in New York City. Or why not acquire Rosalyn L. Bruyere's *Wheels of Light,* designated by *Meditation Magazine* as "a remarkably precise introduction to the intuitive and scientific study of the human aura"? Or how about *Up Your Punctu-*

ation, a simple guide to upgrading your punctuation skills, to which the only possible response must be "No, up yours!" There's available a volume of poetry, *The Lion's Tears,* which "presents the realities of the librarian's soul." (Gustave Flaubert, where are you when we need you?)

A title like that brings us close to the real pathetic bottom of the BAD book trade, vanity publishing, whose sad but egotistic suckers are moved to extraordinary excitement by ads headed

AUTHORS WANTED BY NEW YORK PUBLISHER

(And if that *New York* don't fetch 'em, as Twain's Duke would say, "I don't know Arkansaw.") Counting on readers' innocence about what *subsidy* means, the ad goes on:

> Leading subsidy book publisher seeks manuscripts of all types: fiction, non-fiction, poetry, scholarly and juvenile works, etc. New authors welcomed.

Of course new authors are "welcomed," for they will not be likely to know that *subsidy* means that they will lay out a lot of money to get their clumsy, pitiful, unpublishable stuff printed and bound and stacked up in a warehouse (storage charges paid monthly by author) or sent them in heavy cartons (freight charges paid by author) to repose forever in the attic.

This publisher contracts to "advertise" his list, and that word prompts titillating fantasies of celebrity and success. Every week, thus, in a large New York newspaper appears an ad offering books like these, just as if someone might want to buy them:

A BOX OF CHALK FOR GOLDILOCKS

> An engaging novel that brings to life all the joy, pain, and frustration of teaching. $13.95

JOKES: CLEAN, DIRTY, AND RAUNCHY

A compendium of the best jokes for all tastes—from
the tame to the risqué. $8.95

WITHIN AND WITHOUT—GRAVITY PERSISTS

Controversial food for thought that may shake physics
as we know it. $7.95

WANDERINGS

An inspiring and thoughtful journey into the joys of
self-discovery. $6.95

And some of these little ads, written by a tongue-in-cheek
copywriter who must despise himself or herself anew each
week, are too touching for satire, like

POEMS FOR MY BELOVED

A beautiful bouquet in verse honoring the poet's late
wife of thirty years. $10.00

and

PLANT ME SOME FLOWERS AND CHOKEBERRY TREES

A True Story

A mother's poignant tribute to her teenaged daughter
who died in a tragic accident. $13.95

It's probably unnecessary to emphasize the moral status of
entrepreneurs who would take easy advantage of such de-
fenseless deprivation and simplicity, and it's a pleasure to
note that one company which has flourished for years with
this conscienceless racket has recently been convicted of

fraud—for telling its poor dupes that their books would be promoted through bookstores—and heavily punished. But one can be certain that that company will spring back to rejoin the ranks of the numerous other subsidy publishers.

A long American cultural continuity is represented by this screw-the-suckers BAD-book trade. Well over a half century ago, Hemingway, in *In Our Time,* was sending up a pathetic upper-class "poet" who was victimizing himself like these less well positioned patsies. Living in France with other artistic phonies, he found that he "had nearly enough poems for a book now. He was going to bring it out in Boston and had already sent his check to, and made a contract with, a publisher." (The story is "Mr. and Mrs. Elliot," and it holds up remarkably well. The reason may not be far to seek. There will never be any trustworthy international statistics, but I'd be willing to bet that, given appropriate relative-population adjustments, the United States leads the world in this vanity-publishing scam. The whole horrible act is a testimony to the need of Americans, who tend to believe that everything is attainable if you'll just learn the ropes, to lunge at any slick opportunity for distinction and celebrity.)

But such warnings against BAD books like these won't protect a reader against the really BAD ones, which like blockbuster movies (see *BAD Movies*) are hyped almost past one's will to resist. When Orwell indicated how "bad" the majority of books are, his lowercase *bad* practically summed up the matter, for the commercial tradition of the annual really BAD big book was just getting started. Grace Metalious's *Peyton Place* (over 9 million copies sold) and William Blatty's *The Exorcist* (over 12 million) were still waiting in the wings. But progress cannot be stopped, and by now BIG BAD books—those immense, everlasting, weighty novels that middle-class people like to be seen toting around—are specifically the commodities that keep numerous publishers from foundering, and only one per season, if it catches on, will be enough to do the trick.

For years the industry has puzzled over the question of why people acquire these wordy, overstuffed, great big thick novels promising a protracted read lasting from September ("the fall list") until June or July. The best answer: if you read only one book a year, and you're proud of it, you want that one *to look like a book*—thick, hardbound, serious, one to be seen with on bus, train, or plane, or on the street, and one so heavily advertised and well known that your owning a copy will proclaim your solid location in the main line of consumers. *You are doing it right,* and that's not just a comfort, it's an intense satisfaction. Whether a hypertrophied production of Danielle Steel, Scott Turow, or Herman Wouk, the BIG BAD blockbuster will have prepared its way, rather like John the Baptist with Jesus, by a multimillion-dollar ad and publicity blitz. After that, who can tell or who really cares what the book's really like? And as with the movie industry, the expensive hardbound book is not always the most important commodity being sold: the subsidiary rights (first and second serial, movie, stage, audiocassette, TV, T-shirt, etc.) often bring in more money.

Novelist and scriptwriter Larry McMurtry has had the wit to notice that "it is really reductive to call what we have now a 'publishing industry,' when what it is is a media complex, in which promotability, not literary merit, is the *sine qua non.*" Thus, a guarantee of BIG BAD books for many years to come, enough to make us wish we were stuck with only BAD ones.

BAD CITIES

The cities' need to avert bankruptcy by extravagant tourist-enticing publicity has turned cities that used to be bad into impressive examples of BAD. Washington, D.C., used to attract spenders by stressing its monuments and political features. Now it feels obliged to present itself as a locus of taste and sophistication, even though it has little theater, minimal music, a second-rate newspaper, complete with horoscopes and funnies (see *BAD Newspapers*), and virtually no literary life. It likes to assert that the presence of all those embassies gives it an exciting international flavor, but it hopes we don't know that the occupants of embassies and consulates all over the world are very dull people, the sort you might find at, say, field-grade rank in the world's armed forces, relishing the security of the obedience culture and quite devoid of originality, wit, or charm.

It would not be easy to specify the American cities that would rank high in the BAD competition. There are so many in the running. Atlantic City and Las Vegas would be well up in the list, although they are really not much worse than some others, like Miami Beach, Miami (a national violent-crime city), and Tampa, Florida; Camden, New Jersey; Pierre, South Dakota; Juneau, Alaska; Yuba City, California; Pine Bluff, Arkansas; Albany, Georgia; Gadsden, Alabama; Fitchburg, Massachusetts; Lawton, Oklahoma; Lantana, Florida (home of the *National Enquirer*); and Pascagoula, Mississippi. These are surely bad, but they don't all pretend to be wonderful, and thus they shade away at the bottom of the BAD scale and become simply deplorable. Like places in West Virginia, where the waitress serving you will have no teeth at all and where you will be urged to buy jewelry made of little lumps of coal.

Few places in South Carolina are likely to be very stimulating, for that state's young rack up the lowest SAT scores in the country. In academic distinction it is in competition with Arkansas, which has the lowest teachers' salaries. If you value your health, it would be best not to visit any city in Wyoming, which has no restrictions whatever on handguns, open or concealed. And don't get sick in Odessa, Texas, which has few and archaic medical facilities. Or if you do become unwell there, expect to walk to the hospital, for it also has no public transportation, although its population is over 100,000. In the same way, if you're in or near Athens, Georgia; Bloomington, Illinois; Jacksonville, North Carolina; and twenty-eight other places which might be named, don't expect anything good to eat: according to the *Mobil Travel Guide,* there are no listings for quality restaurants in those cities or their environs. It's hard to imagine what any civilized person might be doing in Salt Lake City, the very pulsating heart of Paphlagonia, but if you should find yourself there, don't try to get a drink, unless you are prepared to exercise extraordinary cunning and alertness.

As the movie *Roger and Me* performed a public service by revealing, Flint, Michigan, is very bad. Its attempts to overcome unfavorable publicity by such acts as burning *Money* magazine—it had designated Flint the worst place in the United States—if they don't at all improve the city, at least move it toward BAD. Travel writers, a cynical and intelligent group, accustomed to producing tongue-in-cheek raves in exchange for free lodging, food, and drink, know as much about both bad and BAD American cities as anyone. They have a name for their members obliged to cover BAD places: shithole specialists. Those are the writers who celebrate not just Atlantic City and Las Vegas but Epcot Center, and who can be brought to rhapsodize about airports and wonderful new multilane highways.

Some places fail to be worthy of the BAD designation because they do not successfully attract a steady supply of costly, empty riffraff, Sinatras and Carol Channings and their riffraff admirers. The question is still unsettled whether Atlantic City or Las Vegas is the best and biggest whorehouse east of Bangkok, but in other respects Las Vegas probably surges ahead. What other city, no matter how awful, has a Liberace Museum, containing the biggest rhinestones in the world?

BAD COLLEGES
AND UNIVERSITIES

About a century ago, Americans set out to experience the higher learning, but after a brief trial, they found they didn't like it. It was too hard and too serious: Latin and Greek took years to learn, and the noble, magnanimous heroes of ancient, medieval, and Renaissance history seemed useless and "irrelevant" as "role models" for the main American activity, making money. An acquaintance with the principles of logic and evidence was found an actual impediment to enthusiasm and good fellowship, and skeptical studies in the history of popular error and the domination of societies by superstition and mobs seemed undemocratic, indeed "elitist." A few genuinely educated people found that precise reasoning and analysis and the disinterested scrutiny of phenomena others uncritically took for granted constituted no formula for gaining "popularity." In short, it was soon discovered that real education was of little value in the American life of action, ambition, acquisitiveness, and getting-on. In fact, just the opposite: the development of intellect led only to an un-American life of study and contemplation.

In the face of these discouraging facts, it's no wonder that Americans devised a reformed system of higher education, one more in keeping with American desires, especially the urge to succeed in public, defined largely as making a pile and living a life untroubled by thought. The invention of intercollegiate athletics was a help here, and so was a new curriculum emphasizing only current events and the techniques appropriate to commercial efficiency. A new subject of study was devised, and it was called "business." Too remote to be useful anymore were history, literature, and philosophy, and such old-fashioned studies also proved too daunting for the untalented masses needed to teach in the public schools. For that reason, another new subject was invented, "education," which, although virtually empty of intellectual content, might allow its dull aspirants to seem engaged in "a course of study" leading to a certified right to teach the young.

The result, visible in all but a few colleges and universities, was the current BAD scene. In fact, it would be hard to find a wider gap between pretension and actuality, the quintessence of BAD, than that in the bulk of these institutions. The folk belief that "going to college" is equivalent to becoming educated is precious to Americans, and the prevailing egalitarianism leads them to treasure "a college degree" without the unpleasant critical work required to distinguish one college degree from another. But the disturbing fact is that earning a bachelor's degree from Williams, Amherst, or Smith should never be confused with receiving one from, say, Middle Tennessee State University or Hawaii Pacific College. There is irony and pathos in the way so many BAD institutions became emplaced, largely during the Kennedy and Johnson administrations. The goal was to widen access to "educational opportunity," and in pursuit of this end verbal inflation (see *BAD Language*) was called on to promote to university status numerous normal schools and teachers colleges, business academies, secretarial institutes, provincial theological seminaries, and trade schools. The technique was not to turn them into universities—too laborious, and it would take decades, if not centuries—but simply to call them universities. These are the places that now award "college degrees" to the majority of young Americans, but the degrees measure not the development of intellect but the rude command of techniques likely to fit the recipients uncritically into the ready-made niches of American middle-class society. Twenty-four percent of American bachelor's degrees are in "business," and more master's and doctor's degrees are awarded in "education" than in anything else.

And even if you've "majored" in business, chances are you'll be too illiterate to be very good even at that. "Do You Know These Words?" asks an ad for a set of "Career Success Vocabulary Cassettes" which teach you not merely what "800 valuable words" mean but supply "two business-oriented sentences" to illustrate each. That this is aimed at the "educated" is clear from the ad's asserting that these cassettes provide "a college experience after college." And what are these difficult words for which post-"collegiate" study is required? They include *transcend, stratagem, efficacy, laconic, ubiquitous,* and *fait accompli,* which might be thought the very stones and mortar of a test designed to exclude unready high school students from college admission. The people who don't know these words have all graduated from universities, and many have gone on to earn their doctorates—in education. In Iowa the most popular professional degrees are not in medicine or law. Forty-one percent are in chiropractic.

If you have an instinct for irony and sometimes need

to relieve a gloomy day with a laugh, you might copy out the next sentence and tape it to your bathroom mirror. The Associated Press reported recently, in an article some newspapers exultantly headlined

MORE AMERICANS ARE BETTER EDUCATED,

that one-fifth of Americans over the age of twenty-five have completed "four years of college." Great news, until you try to find someone who's read anything but a best-seller, who has an iota of historical imagination, or who manifests curiosity about anything but money, sports, "entertainment," or hobbies. What the AP means is that more Americans than ever have attended business school or sat through classes in "education," hardly cause for celebration or national self-congratulation. Yet the self-congratulation is inevitable when would-be encouraging words like the following, from a national newspaper, raise no eyebrows and occasion no cynical smiles:

> Universities in Europe used to have reputations, at least in the United States, as ivory towers whose walls would never be sullied by the corporate world. Many Europeans prided themselves on that ideal, equating it with intellectual integrity.
>   That has changed.

That is, the American work of transforming education into mere training, and at institutions that are largely the uncritical creatures of corporations, has now spread all over the world, and we're all better off. "At our best, at the best 300 colleges and universities in this country, we . . . remain the envy of the world. . . ." That's what Sol Gittleman, provost of Tufts University, proclaimed recently. Apparently there was no one nearby to be quoted commenting, "Poor world!"

Although the United States doesn't really want the higher learning—too difficult, too useless, too alienating —it must pretend to want it, for even a simulacrum of it is still excellent for prestige. Even if most American universities are hardly loci of thought at all but rather costly sports centers and health spas, the demands of pretension determine that the word *university* be attached to everything that might conceivably bear it, even as the real thing grows more and more rare. Certain states used to award the titles *college* and *university* critically and skeptically, but now you can attach those words to virtually anything without shame or fear of legal action. After all, the only people you are screwing are the innocent.

The state of Virginia is one where it is apparently easy to invoke these misleading terms: consider TV evangelist Pat Robertson's "CBN University" at Virginia Beach and Jerry Falwell's "Liberty University" at Lynchburg. Falwell's operation, now the largest private "university" in Virginia, is a good example of unearned promotion by renaming: as late as 1983 it still adhered to some elementary standards of honesty, calling itself Liberty Baptist College. It hadn't yet elevated itself into pretended parity with real universities, identifiable as places inviting the free play of the skeptical mind over all subjects without regard for the consequences. There is actually one "university" in the Middle West which announces that it accepts only "Christian" students willing to abjure dancing, gambling, smoking, drinking, and swearing. Chapel attendance is compulsory, and most of its degrees are in (surprise!) "education."

Actually, the word *university* has been stained so grievously by institutions like that, and like Oral Roberts University Tulsa, Oklahoma, and Bob Jones and Brigham Young, that it might be best if genuine universities now dropped the term and became content to be named simply Yale, Harvard, Princeton, Stanford, and the like. This would be hard, admittedly, on California, Pennsylvania, Chicago, Michigan, and Virginia, but some substitute could be found, the way the Sorbonne (formally, the University of Paris) found one.

The lower reaches of the higher learning are so BAD that one doesn't expect anything below them. But the diligent student of BAD will not be disappointed, for below the hopeless colleges and universities there is a whole raft of worse ones, where there is no relation at all between the apparent and the actual. One measure of a genuine university, and of a good restaurant as well, is that it does not advertise. But it is on advertising alone that truly BAD universities wholly depend. It's interesting that airline magazines, especially, swarm with ads for universities promising bachelor's, master's, and doctor's degrees in return for cash payments and depositions about one's "life experiences." These ads openly equate possession of these degrees with business success, which means (unearned) promotion to executive status. Thus "Nova University," Fort Lauderdale, Florida, exhorts the dark-suited, white-shirted, ambitious, but professionally frustrated air traveler to add "Doctor" to his titles:

> Earn your Ed.D. without Interrupting
> Your Career.

The pathologist of American intellectual geography can't help noticing how many of these enterprises are sited in California, which has provided space, legal freedom, and ample credulity for

Union University
South Union Graduate School
Southwestern University
American Western University

and many others, although the University of Beverly Hills apparently went too far in some direction or other and is now defunct. The only better place, perhaps, to establish fake universities is Hawaii, which at least until 1988 had no laws prohibiting such rip-offs. Florida is another favorite location for vanity universities. Perhaps California, Hawaii, and Florida are favored for these swindles not just because of their weak or nonexistent laws prohibiting fraud, but because in those sunny, optimistic places the outside is regularly valued over the inside, the appearance over the actuality. Hence phenomena like Hollywood, Ronald Reagan, etc. And if you think the BAD situation in America is bad (over half a million of our fellow citizens now "hold" these fake degrees), consider India and Colombia. India has several phony universities openly selling medical degrees to all comers, while at last report Colombia could boast no fewer than fifty-six bogus universities (twenty-seven in Bogotá alone) granting unearned diplomas upon payment of high fees. (For more on this depressing but illuminating subject, see David W. Stewart and Henry A. Spille, *Diploma Mills: Degrees of Fraud* [New York, 1988].)

But you don't have to stir around in that muck to find evidence of BAD. There's plenty up at the middle stratum. BAD colleges and universities are those whose faculties bear elegant titles and at commencement appear in flashy gowns and hoods, but whose students do not learn foreign or ancient languages, the history and principles of philosophy, and the techniques of thought, gaining their degrees by accumulating "credits" in various unrelated, and usually trivial, subjects, most of them involving the sort of current events studied in high school. BAD colleges and universities finally extrude with impressive credentials students whose essays, if any, have never received rigorous criticism requiring them to revise substantially. BAD colleges and universities consist of students (and certainly faculties) devoid of curiosity except where it can be shown to result in academic promotion. There is one university in the Northeast whose ability to teach its students the fundamentals of intellectual honesty can be gauged from its renaming its department of physical education the Division of Human Kinetics.

BAD colleges and universities create students who automatically join the labor force without the capacity to wonder what they're doing or whether their work is right or wrong, noble or demeaning. Habituated to BAD themselves, they grow up to constitute the audience and future clients of BAD everywhere. And a great many of them, having no intellectual interests, manifest their loyalty to their institution by becoming, in due course, "Boosters"— those vain, cunning, immature, and crooked donors to their college's system for dishonestly supporting unqualified, fraudulent student-athletes. In June 1990, the *Chronicle of Higher Education* published a rundown of colleges recently exposed and humiliated for violations of NCAA rules they had publicly agreed to honor. Their behavior resulted in rebukes, suspensions, forfeitures of past victorious sports records, probation, cutoff of future TV appearances, reduction of scholarships, restitution of money dishonestly acquired, barring of coaches from off-campus recruiting, and cancellation of current sports seasons. It is to be noted that the *Chronicle of Higher Education* is not, at least openly, a satiric journal, and it normally does not set out to ridicule the world it reports. But here a reader would not have to be terribly bright or skeptical or sardonic to appreciate the horrible joke. These institutions are denominated "universities": now, if the court please, I ask you to try to imagine an athlete gaining an education in ethics at these places. This is the *Chronicle*'s Dishonor Roll:

Adelphi University
Alabama A&M University
Arizona State University
University of Cincinnati
Clemson University (which has just brought American
    culture to the Soviet Union by establishing the
    first business school there)
Cleveland State University
Eastern Kentucky University
Florida A&M University
Grambling State University
Houston Baptist [!] University
University of Houston
University of Kansas ("lack of institutional control" of
    the athletic program, notes the *Chronicle*)
University of Kentucky
Marshall University
University of Maryland at College Park ("lack of insti-
    tutional control . . . unethical conduct by four
    former coaches and staff members")
Memphis State University
University of Minnesota–Twin Cities ("lack of institu-
    tional control")
North Carolina State University
University of Oklahoma
Oklahoma State University
Robert Morris College (a business school near Pitts-
    burgh: "improper aid to a men's basketball player;
    lack of institutional control")
University of South Carolina
Southeastern Louisiana University
Southern Methodist University ("pattern of repeated
    rules violations")
State University of New York/College at Plattsburgh
Texas A&M University
West Texas State University,

and this list barely suggests the dimensions of the BAD-
ness. In the same issue of the *Chronicle* we find:

Coach Admits Giving Money to
Central Wash. U. Players for Years. . . .

. . . When an internal audit revealed that [this basketball coach] had distributed $65,000 . . . to the players
on his teams, university officials reacted with
alarm. . . . Thousands of people . . . say they support
[the coach; the coach insists he gave athletes money
only as wages for work they did . . . or as loans the
players were to pay back through work . . .]. How, they
wonder, can actions that are so clearly benevolent be
viewed as improper?

But despite the NCAA sanctions, the creeps are not slow in
worming themselves back in. Just recently, the coaches at
Southern Methodist, punished severely for numerous cynical violations, managed to suggest that they now be allowed
to take part in admissions discussions, adding their brute
voices to those of the presumably learned and civilized.

The lack of intellectual distinction at the bulk of these
"schools"—correct term—is obvious, but on the basis of
this showing a further most serious warning may be appropriate:

PARENTS!

If you don't want to cheat your children, if you want
them to be honest, independent-minded, brave,
thoughtful, and self-respecting, *under no circumstances
let them attend any of these institutions,* where they are
likely to learn little but the art of athletic boostership
and master the skill of winking at the authorities.

And it's not the badness that's so appalling; it could be said
that in this country, that's expected. It's the BADness, the
pretense that these institutions are real universities, hon-

orable, learned, incorruptible, somehow a beacon to society because of their pursuit of disinterested scholarship. Real BAD.

Addendum on BAD Academic Costume

Time was when academics in procession wore sober black gowns and traditional square mortarboards, with only hoods—n.b., not *sashes*—providing here and there spots of color signifying their degrees and the institutions awarding them. In those days, people tended to know that academic wear was a *gown,* not a *robe*—hence the Town vs. Gown cliché: robes, they knew, were for judges. But now, what with the breathtaking multiplication of colleges and universities and the wild increase in the numbers that have loitered through them, few know what to call these things, or many other things, just as they've not heard of Chapman's *Homer* or Spinoza or the Great Chain of Being. Now that simplicity has grown suspect, pretentiousness and meaningless fanciness have replaced the old solemnity and dignity. Just as in acting and conversation (see *BAD Conversation*) a sophisticated understatement is rare today, now when you see an academic procession, what you behold is largely BAD.

Harvard must bear much of the blame here, for it began the Modern Movement in academic costume, granting its doctors, of philosophy and other things, the right to wear pinkish (in its view, *crimson*) gowns with contrasting black velvet stripes on the sleeves. Immediately, the floodgates opened, and soon the worst universities were giving their doctors the gaudiest gowns. The mortarboard seeming now hopelessly out of date, little square tams were devised, and some very BAD institutions came out with immensely wide pseudo-Elizabethan hats—unwittingly comic when worn by professors of accounting and marketing, whose command of Renaissance things is such that the King James version is quite beyond their comprehension.

Because the former dignified black doctor's gown favored by Harvard before the color revolution bore on its two front velvet panels tiny embroidered frogs colored to indicate the field of the degree (blue for "Philosophy," etc.), it soon became clear that you could embellish those panels with all sorts of logos and signifiers—university "arms" and seals (all of course bogus in their own right) and obvious emblems of various kinds—and before long doctors from Columbia sported two matched crowns in front, Rutgers (once Queen's College) two hideous little italic capital Q's with "1766" underneath, the University of Michigan two little lamps of learning (get it?), Boston University its flashy, tasteless seal, etc. The costumers of divines were not slow to follow the trend, and now you see ministers sporting gowns bearing on the front panels a matched set of those classic middlebrow praying hands of Albrecht Dürer—to make sure the congregation catches on. The whole phenomenon illustrates the essence of BAD: overstatement and simpleminded literalism, like the irrelevant invocation of color to jazz up classic movies or to recommend news photos to the vulgar.

BAD CONVERSATION

Although now endemic and worldwide, there's little doubt that BAD conversation makes its home in the United States. In a country where medical evidence indicates that one in ten persons, on average, is quite insane, BAD conversation is no surprise. And in a country which values loud noise as much as this one, requiring one to engage in shouting, with attendant overstatement and the disappearance of subtlety, suggestiveness, wit, and irony, BAD conversation is almost an obligation if you want to communicate at all. And for most people, it's a pleasure— they have so little opportunity to assert themselves and thus achieve a bit of selfhood and some small illusion of power. But it's really a question whether the noise causes the BAD, high-volume conversation, or whether the conversation is so BAD that the noise has to be augmented to drown it out or prevent it entirely. Either way, the two go together, which is why ear-shattering disco music, reggae, and the like are so popular. Who could possibly talk while they are going on? And if you can't talk, you can't reveal how shallow and empty you are. (See *BAD Colleges and Universities.*)

Americans probably interrupt each other in conversation more than other nationals because, in a society of presumed equals, all want to get in their opinion all the time. And no one, of course, listens to anyone else, so important is it to seize the floor. Equally odd, no one really expects addressees to listen either. Over forty years ago Evelyn Waugh, in *The Loved One,* made one of his British residents in California observe a profound truth about Americans, especially those on the West Coast. Sir Francis Hinsley says of his neighbors, "They are a very decent, generous lot of people out here and *they don't expect you to listen.* Always remember that, dear boy." He assures a British friend, "It's the secret of social ease in this country. They talk entirely for their own pleasure. Nothing they say is designed to be heard." What real, collaborative conversation might be Waugh suggests in a reaction to hearing two bores retail long, pointless narratives accompanied with laughter at their own tired jokes. "Of conversation as I love it," he says, "with anecdote occurring spontaneously and aptly, jokes growing and taking shape, fantasy—they know nothing."

The interrupting game is played for its own sake rather than in the interests of any particular point or subject matter. And there are notable gender distinctions, as Barbara Ehrenreich has observed. Men, she finds, interrupt women much more often than they interrupt other men, and much more than women, still timid despite the Movement, interrupt either men or women. Ehrenreich also perceives an increasing impediment to conversation as the former central culture fractures and atomizes, leaving putative conversationalists stranded within their mutually hostile "interest groups." The ever-growing question becomes what to talk about with strangers. There's always the weather, of course, but as Ehrenreich says, unless we can devise "some form of universally understood, content-free, urban small talk," casual conversation will veer inevitably into race or gender offense or the mere registration of individual grievances, political antagonisms, or self-pitying domestic narratives. One convention Americans have developed to keep conversation bland and unthreatening is what British observer Simon Hoggart has called the Geographical Link. This provides the dynamics for energetic talk which can stay well clear of touchy topics. Hoggart illustrates:

> PARTY A: Now, where are you folks from?
> PARTY B: We're from Dayton, Ohio.
> A: Well, is that so? You know, my husband Everett had a cousin—a second cousin, that is—who used to live in Cincinnati, Ohio.
> B: Well, hey, I was in Cincinnati a couple of months back!

And so on. In a geography as extensive as the American, this can go on for hours, and very satisfyingly too. Thank God for it, for without it it would take only a few moments for one speaker to ascertain that the other has an absolutely criminal attitude about

Whales
Dolphins
The homeless
Abortion
The denial of tenure to some quite distinguished
    young college teacher
The terrible way women are treated everywhere

and further conversation would be impossible. As it is, in BAD conversation, anger and envy are always on the verge of bursting out. There seems a constant agitation toward something powerful but not expressed, some frustration— perhaps of American dreams and implicit promises cruelly broken. Is the cause a persisting disappointment in the way life has turned out? Whatever the reason, BAD conversation seldom touches on objective phenomena unrelated to the self. It dwells all but exclusively on personal desires and images, and for all its offensiveness, is really an unvoiced cry for help. Which although touching, does not make it any less boring.

BAD ENGINEERING

If pressed, Americans may admit that the ideas that have made the modern world have all originated elsewhere—ideas like Darwin's and Marx's and Freud's and Einstein's and Jung's—and never in These States. Our forte, which compensates for our weakness in creative intelligence, is held to be engineering. Perhaps deficient in a comprehensive understanding of values and ends, we are said to be gifted in the management of techniques and means.

And that's a plausible conclusion. American success in devising passenger aircraft and selling them to the world's airlines, as well as placing men on the moon, has given the impression that Americans are good at engineering and building things. But actually, they're about as good at that as, say, at controlling infant mortality, stopping murder in Washington, D.C., or establishing public medical insurance. And yet the bragging goes on, with the self-congratulation seldom shaken by actualities. The way people talk, you'd think no one in the United States had ever ridden a Japanese or a French fast train—a French one runs safely at 320 miles an hour. And you'd think that everyone had chosen to forget that the Concorde is a French and British, not an American, achievement, and that Velcro was contrived not by a Yank but by a Swiss bright enough to wonder why burrs adhered to his socks. The American achievement—I know it's bad taste to mention this—is the *Challenger,* brought to you by faulty manufacture, inept and dishonest quality control, and lying and evasion for the sake of big bucks.

Another American achievement is the showy and dramatically expensive Hubble Space Telescope ($1.5 billion), for years an occasion of national self-praise and complacency. But when deployed in June 1990, it proved not to work, as a result of what the press called "flawed mirrors" (that is, ground to the wrong curvature), "an embarrassment," said one scientific analyst, "to everyone involved in the project." Blame for this most bizarre fiasco passed rapidly back and forth among several manufacturers and suppliers and inspectors and NASA, leaving what a commentator termed "an ugly scar" on them all. "It certainly seems strange," said an optical expert, "that a project of that magnitude ended up with a flaw like this." But it will seem less strange the more we notice the BAD distance between pretense and actuality in American engineering and construction. Every day brings a new depressing headline, like this:

A WIDELY USED TREATED PLYWOOD IS FOUND TO DECAY IN A FEW YEARS

Faults in Roof Material Are Prompting Lawsuits

or:

SOARING COSTS OF ASBESTOS REMOVAL FORCE
HARD CHOICES ON MANY SCHOOLS

or:

ACID PAPER RUINING HALF THE BOOKS IN
RESEARCH LIBRARIES

People as materialistic as Americans are supposed to be gifted at material operations, but the local urge toward the showy and spectacular constantly invites disaster. As in the collapse in 1978 of the vainglorious wide-span, computer-designed roof of the Hartford Civic Coliseum— and the next year the similar pratfall of the roof of the costly Kemper indoor arena in Kansas City, five years after that building had won a design prize from the American Institute of Architects. This sort of thing is now common, until today there are approximately five hundred similar embarrassments annually. A few more: the collapse in 1983 of the whole ceiling of the classy new Journal Square Center for rail commuters in New Jersey. Fifty tons of stuff fell on a crowd, killing two and injuring eight. Later, the roof of the Silverdome Stadium, in Pontiac, Michigan, collapsed *for the second time* because it could not support the weight of a Michigan snowstorm.

Bad design and construction, in fact, appear to the rest of the world to be something like American specialties. Recently the Army Corps of Engineers inspected almost 4,000 dams—those considered most in danger of coming apart. Of those, 988 proved "unsafe" and 58 "urgently unsafe"—that is, move if you live near one. People living below the Teton Dam in Idaho didn't move in time in June 1976. When it gave way, it killed 11 persons, injured 2,000, and caused over $1 billion worth of damage.

Five years ago American highway bridges were inspected: over 40 percent were found "deficient." One in Connecticut collapsed in 1983, killing three people who trusted it. Four years later, it was New York State's turn: ten people were killed when a bridge on the Thomas E. Dewey Thruway collapsed. To be sure, the inevitable natural erosion of the "infrastructure" causes some of this, but unimaginative engineering and dishonest contracting must share the blame—that is, unless all these dams and bridges were designed and built by Americans of uncommon ability and probity. It's useful for everyone to know that in the ruins of some failed structures investigators have found embedded in the concrete workmen's lunchpails, articles of clothing, trash, cans, bottles, and other nonfunctioning items not counted on by architects and engineers.

Not to be forgotten are the leaks in the roof of the Kennedy Center in Washington (it cost $4 million to repair them), the failure of the pretentious marble-slab walls of the Lyndon Johnson Library in Austin, Texas (the grouting proved ill-mixed), and the similar disaster to the marble surface of the Motor Vehicle Building in the grandiloquent Rockefeller Mall in Albany, resulting in a $25 million suit against the general contractor and designers. Well known is the behavior of the glass panels on the sixty-two-story John Hancock Building in Boston. After a number of the panels fell off, seriously endangering pedestrians below, it was found that the glass wasn't strong enough. All the panels, more than 10,000 of them, were replaced, at a cost of over $8 million. Then it was found that the building needed some additional bracing against the wind: it swayed ominously. That cost $17.5 million more. So numerous and grand have been the resulting lawsuits that only lawyers have come out ahead. Hancock has sued the glass company, the architect (the noted I. M. Pei), and the contractor, all of whom are suing someone else back. The cost of the whole performance is estimated at over $100 million.

"Smug" is the word invoked by Paul Weidlinger, a leading structural engineer, to designate the complacent attitude about one's own adequacy that underlies these bizarre events. Add smugness to laziness, ignorance, and defect of imagination and you have all the requirements for BAD. A combination of un-adult optimism and commercial disingenuousness lies behind frequent disasters which can be handily blamed on "the weather." In *Fortune* magazine, Walter McQuade quotes one architect who lays much of the blame correctly on the inaccurate specifications for their products issued by manufacturers. "A tragic joke," he says, "is equating high performance in a wall with withstanding the pressure of a forty-two-mile wind . . . when we know that almost all cities have seventy-mph winds on occasion." The point was illustrated recently when children were killed by the wall of a school building which fell on them in an "unexpectedly" high wind.

American metallurgy, given our long experience with steel, would seem to be one of our strong suits. It might be thought, for example, that the bolts we use for building must be about the best in the world. Quite wrong. It was in part the failure of the suspension rods that caused the collapse of the roof of the Kansas City arena, just as in that unfortunate city it was the failure of the bolts that helped cause the fall of the showy walkways over the lobby of the Hyatt Regency Hotel, where 114 people died. Unsuspected weakness in the bolt holding a jet engine to an aircraft wing caused the crash of a DC-10 at Chicago in 1979, an event catastrophic for the book trade: many of the 273 killed were flying to a publishers' convention on the West Coast.

It's become so bad that media people could save time by having on their word processors a way of printing not the individual letters but the whole word *collapse*:

Brownsville, Texas: "At least 11 people are dead
in the collapse of a roof."

New York City: "31st St. Building Collapse
Stops Subways and Trains and Hurts 10."

Green Bank, West Virginia: "Giant Telescope Collapses: Big U. S. Research Setback."

Covington, Tennessee: "Bridge Collapses. Seven
Fall to Death."

Long Beach, California: "No one knows what
prompted the collapse on July 2 [at California State
University]. . . . The recital hall . . . was empty when
120 tons of steel and concrete fell to the ground, crush-
ing two grand pianos."

Ruins would be another useful logotype, as in this photo
caption:

A 20-ton scoreboard lies in ruins on the floor of the
new $52 million coliseum in Charlotte, N.C. . . . The
scoreboard, which cost $1.2 million, fell . . . yesterday
as it was being lifted to the ceiling. . . .

Chaos is a word which we will also be seeing a lot of:

COMPUTER CHAOS FOR AIR TRAVELERS

May 13, 1989. The nation's largest airline computer
reservation system . . . inadvertently shut down for almost 12 hours yesterday, disrupting the operations of
about 14,000 travel agencies nationwide.

What a great idea it was to bury the tanks holding
gasoline at gas stations and cleaning fluid at dry cleaners:
entirely avoids the hazards of aboveground storage, where

every spark or struck match risks an explosion. In Southern California, however, the failure to imagine the inevitable rusting and corrosion of these tanks has resulted in the widespread contamination of drinking water. Some examples, from the *Los Angeles Times*:

> Davis: A service station leak of 35,000 gallons of gasoline contaminated [a] city well 100 yards away.

> Glenville, Kern County: Gasoline contamination of seven wells . . . was discovered along a quarter-mile swatch . . . in 1985.

Buried tanks of cleaning solvents deteriorate too:

> Modesto: Four tanks at old laundry leaked solvent into soil and groundwater . . . prompting a $1 million municipal cleanup.

And so on. It might not be going too far to suggest that if the people responsible were educated as well as trained (see *BAD Colleges and Universities*), they might have more elastic imaginations, able to foresee the future of their tanks, and they might also develop a loyalty to things and people other than oil companies and gas stations.

In the same way, the people building and maintaining nuclear-energy and nuclear-weapons plants might have looked at broader perspectives than the contemporary "threat of foreign oil" or megatonnage absurdities and considered local leukemia rates. The situation is too depressing to go into here, but anyone interested in the appalling nuclear dimension of BAD engineering and construction may consult Teddy Milne's *The Unseen Holocaust: A Sad Record of Nuclear Accidents, Leakages, Mismanagement and Cover-ups* (1987). It is to engineers, after all,

that we owe the scandal of nuclear waste disposal, which
no one seems to have thought much about when the whole
mad enterprise was complacently begun. But in America
there's a small comfort. There's a built-in defectiveness in
most engineering enterprises that constitutes a surprise
silver lining. It was found recently, for example, that one-
third of the MX missiles were either unusable or would
never reach their targets, thus taking numerous terrified
Europeans off the hook and exposing the pretension to
engineering excellence on which the preposterous American position in the Cold War has depended.

That's simply a national or international magnifica-
tion of the New York City problem with its highly touted
new buses, the Grumman Flxibles (*sic*: a typical cuteism;
see *BAD Language*). These were cleverly designed to save
fuel, to be accessible to the handicapped, to be comfortably
air-conditioned and electronically controlled. Their light-
weight frames, however, almost immediately developed fa-
tigue cracks and steering anomalies, and the New York
Transit Authority finally dumped the whole package of
637 buses, saying good-bye to $92 million.

Looking for the causes of that gaffe and many others,
one should never underestimate the contribution of the
national illiteracy. People need manufacturing and construction jobs, and to get them they must pretend to read
specifications and follow written instructions. Of course
many have to fake it, and bridges and ceilings collapse,
welds (as on the Alaska Pipeline) prove insufficient, and
things in general don't work. As Walter McQuade says,
"The ironic truth is that we live in an age of great technological talent but waning on-the-job competence." Another
way of putting it would be to point out that a pretentious
technology is outpacing the human ability to manage it, or
even to be very skeptical about it.

Probably few would want to return to the encourage-

ments to competence specified in the Code of Hammurabi
(c. 1750 B.C.):

> If a contractor builds a house for a man and does not
> build it strong enough, and the house which he builds
> collapses and causes the death of the house owner,
> then the contractor shall be put to death.

> If it causes the death of the son of the owner, then the
> son of the contractor shall be put to death.

But that draconic solution at least would help avoid the
common American outcome of construction failures, the
enrichment of lawyers.

Finally, it's important to understand that engineering
and construction are equally bad elsewhere (recent head-
line: "100 Die as India Train Falls off Bridge"). But if bad,
it is not BAD. Nobody ever said that India was a gung-ho
technological marvel and therefore the envy of the rest of
the world. (And see *BAD Architecture*.)

BAD FILMS

Films? *Films?* A pretentious word. See *BAD Movies*.

BAD FOOD

An immense subject in America, to be sure, but manageable if bad food—rutabagas and Jell-O, for example—is carefully distinguished from BAD. Food writer Coleman McCarthy has helped define BAD food by emphasizing that in fruits and vegetables, "pretty" has overtaken actual, honest, and safe in the Basic American Diet, which, conveniently for us, he abbreviates B.A.D. What he's getting at is the scandal of cosmeticizing produce to make it attractive to the ignorant—coloring oranges orange, for instance, or breeding apples and cherries and strawberries so impressively large that they're quite tasteless. Now, in violation of all natural laws, "Apples are splotchless, wormless, and lustrously red or green. Grapefruits are perfectly round, as firm as baseballs and as yellow as forsythia," and these phony appearances—BAD in a nutshell—are produced by an infinite number of exotic and untested constituents, residing in the chemicals used to bring on these freaks of visual vegetable perfection.

This manifestation of BAD does accord with the American disinclination to accept unpleasant facts, like the cruel fact that oranges are really greenish-yellow and often ovoid, and the wormless apple is really an anomaly that, without dye and polish, will look pretty shabby. The real thing, here as elsewhere, is thus unacceptable. BAD doesn't just happen. Americans insist on it. Take "processed" cheese. Genuine cheese matures and gradually disintegrates, thus posing what supermarkets managers term a shelf-life problem. If no one objects, or really even notices, why not offer instead processed cheese? Pasteurized as it is, it will last for months. So what if it's bright orange and tastes like putty or something you might encounter in an operating room? If it pretends to be cheese and is accepted as such, that's all that matters.

The American insistence that fruit be prettied up, phonied up, and fancied up is apparent also in the new American way with so classical an item as peanuts. Peanuts themselves are wonderful, but too simple and honest to appeal to contemporary BAD taste. They must be tarted up, sweetened, indeed, by the application of honey, as if we lived in a perpetual nursery or were unable to overcome our childish devotion to Cracker Jack. The much-treasured version now is Honey Roast Peanuts, the equivalent in men's clothing of a dinner jacket made of vermilion velveteen fastened with gilt frogs. Pretzels, whose main merit used to be their saltiness, are now also beginning to appear candy-coated, which makes them, actually, an appropriate accompaniment of American sugary beer, rapidly becoming indistinguishable from diet ginger ale. The taste for "dry" and sour has gone out, and now, lest customers recoil, the Chinese restaurant feels obliged to replace *sweet and sour pork* with *sweet and pungent pork* (see *BAD Language.*) People used to be able to endure a half-second or so of a nonsweet taste when they swallowed an aspirin, but now even aspirin tablets come candy-coated. In fact, *candy-coated* gets close to the essence of BAD, whether food, beliefs, hotels, ideas, restaurants, or television. Yes, "humankind cannot bear very much reality," as T. S. Eliot put it, and with Americans that goes double.

BAD HOTELS

Before the days of Hyatts, Holiday Inns, Marriotts, Howard Johnsons, Ramada Inns, and the like, American hotels used to range from bad to fair. But now, they are almost uniformly BAD. The reason is their grandiloquence, their fondness for putting on airs that don't at all become them. Like "turndown service," the mention of which in its publicity one hotel hopes will occasion a stampede toward its registration desk. Turndown service: that means that between 6:00 and 10:00 P.M. an employee will open *and turn down* your top bedsheet, with attendant blanket. And not just that: she (he? not really plausible) will also deposit two, and sometimes three, individually wrapped *candies* on the turndown. This is what hotel publicity means when it invokes its favorite magic word, *luxury.*

When Donald Trump brags that he is going to turn the Plaza Hotel in New York into "the most luxurious hotel in the world," we know that his idea of "luxury" pivots on nugatory turndowns and unwanted candies at

93

bedtime. And there are further hotel words and ideas which serve as bait for the credulous and unsophisticated. Furnishings are *lush,* drinks *libations, fare* is *exotic,* service *gracious,* settings *elegant.* But lest the socially insecure suffer an attack of nerves when faced with all this unfamiliar *elegance,* one hotel specifies that its dining courtyard is "elegantly casual" (see *BAD Language*), just as a hotel in Honolulu indicates that dress is informal, "except for casually elegant jackets and dresses in the hotel dining rooms at night."

One famous hotel in Washington has achieved the pinnacle of pretentiousness, with strong emphasis on social snobbery and being "correct." It says: "The _____'s distinguished guests come from all parts of the world. They are foreign dignitaries, leaders in government, business, the sciences and the professions. They are men and women accustomed to all the amenities and thoughtful attentions the world can provide." (Like turndowns.) Apparently this hotel's complement of dignitaries and similar classy folks requires instruction in manners and dress, for it issues a little pamphlet of dicta about "certain rules of dress." These are addressed to customers quivering with anxiety lest they fail to do the correct thing—as defined by this hotel. To assist this end, and because staying at this hotel implies "a preference and aptitude for elegant living in the grand manner" (doesn't it make you want to *throw up*?), the hotel management "requests that its guests be decorously attired." And since the name of this hotel constitutes a "correct address," it emphasizes that staying there will impress others and "facilitate one's progress" in getting what one wants out of Washington—like, for example, a Pentagon contract, consummated over BAD booze in a BAD bar, for 100,000 monkey wrenches at $75 each. American hotels, which used to be content to be run by people posing as our employees, are now run by people posturing as our superiors, advisers on correct dress and deportment, even though what they preside over are little more than vertical motels, with such stigmata as ice-cube and vending machines on each floor, free *USA Today* (see *BAD Newspapers*) outside each door in the morning, and constant canned music of the lowest kind.

One notable defect of current American life is that there is virtually no hotel criticism. There seems no one around like, say, H. L. Mencken, secure enough in his standards, contemptuous of money fraud, and uncowed by pretense, to comment justly on hotels. In 1946, he said of a well-known hotel in Washington, which most people found not just satisfactory but actually grand, "The _____ is probably the worst hotel on earth, though one of the most pretentious. It is full of gadgets marked 'For Your Protection'—bags to hold drinking-glasses, paper tapes over the toilet bowls, etc.—but its comforts are very meagre." And it's gotten worse since Mencken's day. What would he say of valet parking (see *BAD Restaurants*)? How would he react to being invited to ride in a hotel limousine instead of a taxi with no mention of price, and then be charged $30 at his destination? What would he say about the three-quarter-hour wait for the room-service breakfast? The elaborate charade of wine service in the hotel dining room? The long plebeian queues at the checkout counter? The absence of civilized reading matter at the newsstand? (It is said the Mormons managing one BAD hotel chain see to it that the *Atlantic,* the *New Republic,* and *Harper's* make no appearance on its newsstands.) What, indeed, would Mencken say about a maid's barging into his room at 8:30 P.M. to turn down his sheet and blanket and leave there her little individually wrapped candies?

But if hotel criticism is rare today, there is a little, some of it supplied by the estimable Ada Louise Huxtable. "The modern hotel-motel," she observes, "is an almost

symbolic American product," what with its banal standard-
ization, its "bad colors, bad fabrics, bad prints, bad pictures, bad furniture, bad lamps, bad ice-buckets, and bad
wastebaskets, [all displaying] totally uniform and cheap
consistency of taste and manufacture. . . ." The national
uniformity of these bad (no, BAD) things suggests a significant disappearance of alternatives, a satire on the
highly touted American breadth of choice. The fraudulent
illusion of choice prepared by "the hospitality industry" (as
it likes to call itself) resembles the same thing in the TV
industry (see *BAD Television*). And Huxtable goes on to
locate the ultimate model of the "luxury" aped by these
terrible hotels. It derives, she notes, from "every movie of
mythical high life that ever graced the silver screen." As
rendered by hotel planners, architects, designers, decora-
tors, and employees, it comes down to "plastic, mirrors,
and spit," the result of "aesthetic illiteracy and hokey
pretensions"—in short, the distillation of BAD, "an almost
symbolic American product." (And see *BAD Architecture*.)

Another who is unimpressed by hotel pretentiousness
is the writer Mark Randall. It's the greasy-smarmy rhetoric
of the servitors that bugs him. He's thoroughly sick of
hearing in BAD hotels passages like

> "Good evening, sir. And how are you this evening? . . .
> May I get you something from the bar? . . . I'd be
> happy to, sir. . . . And would you care for anything
> else right now? . . . I'll be back with your drink in just
> a moment."

"One wants to say," writes Randall, " 'Well of course you'll
be back with my drink in a moment! SHUT UP ABOUT
IT!' " Randall concludes:

> One sees . . . that this style is designed, not to promote
> service, but to call attention to what we are supposed to

regard as the edifyingly refined manners of the server.
It is the establishment's self-congratulatory way of re-
minding you that you are in a fancy place. . . . What we
have here is neither good manners nor good service; it
is politeness grandstanding, a kind of obsequious bullying.

If mere everyday rudeness is bad, this is BAD, and "an
almost symbolic American product."

BAD IDEAS

Bad ideas are those that are palpably unsound, like constructing a building from the top down, or trying to run a car on water with a pill in it. Some people can always be persuaded to embrace such notions, but most would agree that except as the material of jokes, they are a waste of time. BAD ideas, on the other hand, are widely accepted and so familiar as to go largely unquestioned.

Like the idea that the Postal Service should pay for itself, unlike the Coast Guard, the Air Force, or other essential services. A related BAD idea is that constant postal-rate increases are somehow not a cause of inflation. A further BAD idea, which seldom seems to be called into question, is that access to quality higher education should depend on how much money your father has. Another: that AIDS, homelessness, poverty, and drug addiction are justly punitive, and will probably go away if we do nothing about them. Another: that we don't really need the socialized railway called Amtrak, whose support by federal subsidy does, after all, cut deeply into the profitable business of selling cars.

A BAD idea popular in puritanical and ignorant areas is that the distribution of condoms in high school encourages copulation—all that's wanted will actually take place regardless. The U.S.-quarter-look-alike Susan B. Anthony dollar was a mighty BAD idea, floated by bureaucrats ignorant of Europe and thus unaware that coins of high value must be heavier and of a different *color*, something the British had learned years before. A further BAD idea is that the military should have an influence on foreign or domestic policy, or that military culture should serve as a model for social or political arrangements elsewhere.

Other BAD ideas are popular among academics and those who conceive of themselves as intellectuals. Among such, it's no wonder that the idea of conferences and learned group occasions flourishes: what better way to prevent the hard work of solitary reading, thinking, and writing? People who read a lot but don't write often or very well tend to believe that an author pursues for a lifetime the subject of a book he finished twenty years ago—that is, that he is as dull and static as they are. Intellectuals tend to go in for self-righteous enthusiasms, and it is they (as well as politicians) who lie behind the BAD idea of changing the names of their countries from time to time, making the study of history and geography more difficult than necessary. It is they who decide that Ceylon should now be known as Sri Lanka, Rhodesia as Zimbabwe, and Upper Volta as Burkina Faso. They are the ones lurking behind such BAD ideas as changing Sixth Avenue to "Avenue of the Americas." It is to bright architects, planners, and developers that we owe the BAD idea of suburban streets without sidewalks, an effective discourager of curiosity and exploration, analogous to discouraging serendipitous curiosity in libraries by computerizing the card index.

A lot of BAD ideas, ranging from (as P. J. O'Rourke
has said) Marxism to no-fault auto insurance, result from
"grand theories bearing no relation to reality." A really
BAD idea is buying six cassettes promising to develop your
Power of Self-Esteem, and after listening to them and believing them, conceiving that you are really good. Your friends
will soon indicate how mistaken you are, and then you'll be
back where you started, only poorer by $49.50 + $3.50
shipping charge. "I get some of my best ideas in showers,"
says Arnold Palmer, and they are not lost to humanity,
because there he always has ready his microcassette pocket
recorder, ready to receive his thoughts. All in all, a BAD
idea. But even worse is the fundamental American BAD
idea that writer Jane Walmsley perceives distinguishes us
from all other people, an idea that, as she says, "explains
much superficially odd behavior," like jogging, dieting,
face-lifting, cadaver freezing (*cryonics,* in the trade jargon),
hair-dyeing, and age-despising. "Americans," she perceives, "think that death is optional."

BAD LANGUAGE

It's necessary to understand at the outset that BAD language is not bad, like *shit* or *motherfucker*. It's more like *gaming* for gambling, *taupe* for mouse gray, *starters* for appetizers, *shower activity* for rain, *nonperforming loans* for *bad debts,* and *preexisting* (or *resale*) *home* for used house. That is, there must be in the language, as there is not in, say, *fuck,* an impulse to deceive, to shade the unpleasant or promote the ordinary to the desirable or the wonderful, to elevate the worthless by a hearty laying-on of the pretentious. The object is almost always to make money off the credulous and the insecure, to swindle the naïve and impressionable.

Of course, all the BAD this book has dealt with so far involves, somewhere, pretentious language. This makes it logically hard to devote a distinct section to BAD language alone. Consequently, we will need frequent cross-references, the way the following requires us to see *BAD Colleges and Universities.* For example, professorial BAD:

when a professor refers to his subject as his *discipline*, he's engaging in a sly little gesture of self-praise designed to elevate him (in his view) above someone who's merely curious about something, which he might call a *hobby*, or an *interest*, or even a *field*. *Discipline* is invoked by the professor to show how superior he is to someone who doesn't make a living writing about or at least constantly talking about what only he is interested in. Likewise, *interdisciplinary*, a high-class term heard frequently on the campus, for all its ostentation means only "engaged in by people who are, like most half-intelligent human beings, interested in more than one thing"—or, if you please, not as dull and blinkered as usual. Once you begin saying *discipline* for *field* or *subject*, you may end talking like this ad for one of its books by the Johns Hopkins University Press: " 'Intertextuality,' write the editors, 'simply does not recognize the boundaries of discipline [*what* boundaries?] and is at work in the whole of the world text.' " The pretentiousness there provides all the definition anyone should need of real, downright, 18-karat, 100-proof BAD.

That's not too far removed from the advertising technique used in more coarse environments to flog products. When the radio commercial says, "If you desire to purchase," we recognize a BAD version of "If you want to buy" (see *Bad Advertising*). The untruths at the heart of BAD language sometimes go very far ("You've been a great audience!"), but are no less efficient for that (see *BAD Movie Actors and Other Players*). And why say *customer* when you can say *guest*, and thus deceive some simple soul who will regard bedsheet turndowns and candies as evidence of affection and friendship (see *BAD Hotels*)? Why imply the truth to air travelers by using the word *ditching* when you can substitute *water landing*, or why say *nausea* when you can say *motion sickness* (see *BAD Airlines*)?

Pretentiousness and euphemism are thus the stigmata

of verbal BAD. In a publicly egalitarian society like the American, they offer a special temptation, for here dignity and respect are sought by all but, in their genuine forms, available to few. Alexis de Tocqueville observed of the early United States, "Nowhere do citizens appear so insignificant as in a democratic nation." In this democratic nation, with few possibilities for inherited or *ex officio* signs of personal importance, the quest for individual social significance is unremitting, and if you've not earned it, you can affect it by the means chosen by most Americans, verbal pomposity. When not achieved by a display of euphemisms, dignity, it is thought, can be projected by quantitative means—that is, by adding to the number of syllables required to convey an idea, as if literally adding to its "weightiness." Thus the popularity of *wellness* as a replacement for *health,* the use of *assist* instead of *help, a great dining experience* for *a great dinner, a great reading experience* for *a good read,* etc. Such grandiose syllable augmentation is often combined with euphemistic purpose—*aroma* for *smell,* for example—but more often it's used simply to add weight and number. A *watch* becomes a *timepiece,* just as a *choice* ascends a bit and becomes an *option*—twice as desirable because requiring twice the syllables (see *BAD Advertising*). Outright mention of money constituting, among some people, an offense against gentility, *pay* can be raised to *compensation* and *fee* to *honorarium* (see *BAD Colleges and Universities*). A *pen* is a low, utilitarian thing: to make it more impressive and valuable, call it a *writing instrument.* Among such academics as are given to pretentiousness, the word *method* is not much heard these days. It's now *methodology*: "I approve of his findings, but I'd have used a different research *methodology.*" (The professor saying that can almost certainly be counted on to refer to his subject as his *discipline.*)

   If, tired of one place and anxious to go to another,

you *move,* you are doing something quite unimpressive and insignificant: you can become more important if you *relocate.* Why risk seeming ordinary by saying that you have *decided* when you can say that you have *made a decision,* or better, *made a determination?* Why support some cause or other when you can *be supportive of* it? Why leave a *tip* when you can leave a *gratuity?* Traditionally, newspaper reporters have been represented, as in Hecht and MacArthur's *The Front Page,* as low, vulgar types, given to cynicism, drunkenness, and hat-wearing indoors. To transform them into serious, sober, and valuable "professionals," as well as to imply their employer's hopes that they will display minimal eccentricity and uncontrollability, call them, as an editor of *USA Today* once did, *information delivery systems.* A similar yearning for grandeur turns *rain* into *precipitation,* in theatrical circles *dance* into *movement,* and in business *loss* into *shortfall.*

The fate of the word *salesman* exemplifies both the urge toward high portent and the normal American discomfort in facing unpleasant or demeaning things. Once, a *salesman* was a *salesman,* as in *Death of a,* a useful person, to be sure, but socially low and inclined to make a pest of himself. Or herself, since women were admitted to the occupation, necessitating the welcome addition of a syllable as the word expanded to *salesperson.* In time, more class was felt to be needed, so in due course three syllables were expanded to five *(sales associate)* and then to six *(sales representative).* But this last, it was found, could be extended to eight syllables by designating this person a *merchandising associate,* and the former *sales manager,* a poor thing with only four syllables to his name, was verbally promoted to *vice president, merchandising*—eight syllables, and a nice bit of euphemism as well.

To speak of a *controlled substance* when you mean a *drug* is happily euphemistic, but it also adds three syllables and thus suggests that the speaker has every right to be considered a someone. Since most euphemisms have more syllables than the unbearable words they replace, it is not surprising to come upon *developmentally delayed* to mean what used to be meant by *retarded* or *feebleminded*—a clear gain of four or five syllables. And when a museum wants to get rid of some precious object, it can *de-accession* it: both longer and more evasive than the rude term *sell*.

One unannounced reason behind the movement to change *black* to *African-American* now becomes clear: seven syllables are seven times more impressive than one. I know it will be hard to believe, but in O'Hare Airport, Chicago (see *BAD Airports*), I actually saw this sign on a door leading out to the runways and plane parking spaces:

ALARMED ACCESS DOOR: SECURITY CODE INPUT REQUIRED PRIOR TO EXITING VIA THIS DOOR.

(See *BAD Signs.*) Much grander than "Caution: Opening Door Without Security Code Will Ring Alarm," and certainly more pompous than "For Official Use Only." If the author of the Johns Hopkins University Press ad seems anxious that someone will think him or her merely humanistically educated, the author of the sign on the airport door is working in a similar tradition, one identifiably American—the terrible fear, common in a democracy, of seeming no-'count.

That's a problem especially severe in the military, always doubtful about its social acceptability. Both social-class and euphemistic purposes are served by replacing the simple, honest *war* with *defense* (Department of, Secretary of, etc.). The same with *campaign,* nicer and longer than *war*: "When the campaign is finished . . ." But not all such exercises in syllable multiplication have been successful. The deviser of *human remains pouches* was trying hard, but if his number of syllables is impressive, his coinage hardly succeeds as a euphemism for *body bags.* Not half as winning as *suppressing* a target—that is, destroying it. And for *target,* read group of people, building, or tent village.

BAD language is so much the norm these days that there's virtually nothing said in public that, if both speaker and listener, writer and reader were honest and socially secure, couldn't be moved down toward a modest simplicity. Many of the airlines' usages are euphemistic, to be sure, but many are also in aid of a dignity and complexity presumably worthy of the impressive technological occasion. Like the command, landing being imminent, to "extinguish all smoking materials." Wag Michael Whiteman has commented, "None of my materials are smoking; and as cigars and pipes aren't allowed, why not say cigarettes?" Indeed, why not say "Put out cigarettes now"? Whiteman also notes the pretentiousness of "Please remain seated until the plane has come to a complete stop." "Is not a stop a stop?" he asks. "What is a complete stop?" And the pilot often assures the passengers, "We will be taking off momentarily." He means *soon,* but he can't bear to compromise his dignity by that low term. Why be called an *air waitress* when you can be a *stewardess,* or go all the way to *flight attendant*? That's as good as *disposal* (or better, *recycling*) *engineer* for—shhh!—garbageman.

It's on airlines too that you are likely to find the term *presented* used for purposes which are only pretentious. For example, on an airline menu: "A Selection of Warmed Dinner Rolls Will Be Presented"; normal standards of decency, modesty, and appropriateness would suggest cutting everything except "Rolls" (see *BAD Restaurants, BAD Airlines*). Indeed, *presented* has become a frequent attendant of mock-aristocratic and phony come-ons. One pen company, the one that likes to refer to its products as *writing instruments,* says of one of its (mass-produced) fountain pens that for only $150 you can have it "Presented in a deluxe walnut box"—just as if it were a precious object, really an "art object," and you were a classy connoisseur. (See *BAD Objects.*)

I have descanted elsewhere (in *Class* [New York, 1983]) on the fraudulent use of the word *home* when *house* is meant, an analogue to the fraudulent display of the word *travel* when nothing but *tourism* is meant. Greed motivates both corruptions, on the one hand the greed of "Realtors" (BAD for real-estate agents) hoping to give their commodity a warm, snuggly association, and on the other hand the greed of tour and cruise touters hoping to persuade the innocent that by joining such mass operations they are acquiring the experience of travel. It used to be clearly understood that a *house* and a *home* were different things, which is why there were two different words. Obviously a *housewrecker* and a *homewrecker* are not the same thing, although the new gentility and sentimentality, which impel all sorts of BAD phenomena, are steadily at work effacing such differences. (Does anyone remember when a building lot was honestly so called, and not a *homesite?*) One large newspaper recently allowed itself to fall for the real-estate industry's trick of misnaming houses and to use the term *boarding-homes.* Soon we are sure to hear of *whorehomes, bawdyhomes, homes of prostitution,* and the like. A vast amount of the pathetic American hope, if not assumption, that you can *buy* a good life resides in a statement like "Those people are so lucky: they live in a million-dollar home." Even apartments can now be transformed by BAD language into something they are not. In an ad for one of his apartment houses verbally jazzed up to bear the name "Palace," Donald J. Trump asserts:

Now, at Trump Palace, we have created a series of
palatial homes. Each home has been carefully designed
to fulfill the dreams and desires of those dedicated to
experiencing life at its fullest. . . .
　　　Spectacular views are the hallmark of each
home. . . .

And of course Trump sells *townhomes* as well, formerly
townhouses. (See *BAD Advertising*.) Given this virtual replacement of *house* by *home*, it's not hard to feel some pity
for the magazines *House Beautiful* and *House & Garden*,
stuck forever with those honest titles.

An unearned warm feeling like the one evoked by
home is also a treasured by-product of the BAD word *community*, used when there is no community. Thus *the senior
community* (i.e., old people), *the gay community* (wouldn't
category be better?), *the black* or *Puerto Rican community*, and
so on. As Helen Vendler notes, implicit in the widespread
exhibition of this word is a heavy dose of "false pastoral,"
the same childish, deformed, rose-tinted view of life un-
derlying the constant misuse of *home*. Advertising energet-
ically exploits this sentimentality, and we hear of "a lovely
community of new homes." Anything can be warmed and
sentimentalized by imposing the notion, or at least the
language, of *community* upon it. Thus a writer urging the
appointment of more women professors at the Harvard
Law School says, "The female voice is a relatively new one
in law school communities" (she means law schools). The
ultimate is probably reached in a phrase like *the world community*, usually found in self-righteous and moralistic political contexts: "This blatant [fill in blank with *act of
terrorism, contempt for basic human rights, repression of democratic aspirations*, etc.] will surely be censured by *the world
community*." Speaking specifically of such wishful formula-
tions as *the feminist community*, Vendler correctly observes

that "the utopian and 'touchy-feely' use of the word 'community' . . . can give an outsider the creeps."

Community is a handy little technique of self-praise, but there are many others in the repertory of BAD language. *In-depth* is a prominent one, used most often both to evade precise meaning and implicitly to pat the speaker on the back (see *BAD Advertising*): "This book is based on more than one hundred *in-depth* interviews." (My, how thorough you are!) Likewise, to install the word *concerned* in the designation of any group is a useful way of celebrating the sympathy ("caringness") of its members and implying the coldheartedness of outsiders. Thus members of "Concerned Mothers Against Hepatitis" or "Committee of Those Concerned About Human Rights in Asia" are clearly morally better than those adhering to other groups. In the same way, injecting the term *responsible* into any argument suggests that you are and that your opponent is not.

There is also a collection of BAD words and phrases whose use many hope will bring them a reputation for learning and high sophistication. The cliché *Renaissance man* (to designate someone like Bill Bradley: athlete, Rhodes scholar, senator, etc.) suggests that the speaker knows what he is talking about, indeed, has derived understanding of the term from long and heady contact with the thought of Pico della Mirandola and the writings of Sir Philip Sidney. It's like the charming American habit of naming fraternities and sororities by Greek letters when no one knows any Greek, and hasn't for years, and where people are studying not, as they might like to pretend, philosophy or ancient history (or any other kind) but marketing (formerly *salesmanship*) or "educational psychology."

The pseudo-precision in *Renaissance man* and its corollaries is like that in the famous injunction *Read my lips!*

and the similar quasi-clever phrase *voodoo economics,* useful both for pretension and the avoidance of meaning, since no one has the slightest idea what *voodoo* really means. We owe those memorable phrases to the President who announced recently, as he noticed what was happening in Eastern Europe, "The road to freedom lays before us" (lays *whom?* the impudent will ask). In the same way, *mind-boggling,* invoked frequently, will, it is hoped, bring to the speaker a reputation as a clever phrasemaker. That is the hope also of those who often use the word *dialogue* when they are often talking about merely a conversation, and who hope always for a chance to introduce the phrase *between a rock and a hard place.*

The American lust for dignity and consequence produces daily large yields of comical solecisms. Like *absent* to mean *without* ("Absent further information, we can't tell"), *impact* used as a verb to mean *influence* ("Our campaign didn't seem to impact voters much in Idaho"), *transit* as an elegant synonym for *cross* ("I transited most of Turkey last summer"), and of course that favorite of the bogus and pompous, *parameters* to mean something like *boundaries:* "That new guy doesn't seem willing to work within the company's parameters."

It is sheer BAD that urges so many to say *context* when they mean simply *content, empathy* when they mean *sympathy,* or *concept* when they mean *idea.* Indeed, when someone selling cars, condos, or houses speaks of a new *concept,* it would be well to make sure your wallet is still in place. As counters and emblems in this great American game of unearned cleverness, *meld* for *join* has its attractions, as does the would-be-knowing *mix* for *mixture* and the classy *segue* for *proceed,* or simply *go.* A recent memorable performance in ostentation and consequent collapse was put on by Mr. Andrew A. Alston, a perfectly solid professional, a member of the National Transportation Safety Board.

He was wearing a button-down shirt and the customary "regimental"-striped tie—that is, he looked just like a fully educated and adequate person. He said of a small-plane pilot involved in a puzzling air accident: "I think he wants to find out what happened. . . . That was the attitude he exuded to me."

A bit lower down socially (although one can't be certain about that), it is the new illiteracy that has caused the renaming of the sweetish pink wine that used to be called *rosé*: so many people were humiliated by not knowing whether to say to the waiter *rose-zay* or simply *rose* that they avoided ordering it. Stores and restaurants, catching on, changed its name to *blush*. And just as *rosé* has largely disappeared and *croissant* become almost uniformly *cross-ant,* so Grey Poupon Mustard is now inching toward *Grey Poop-on.* The uncertainties of higher education these days (see *BAD Colleges and Universities*) make it more likely than ever that the specialists in rhetoric who devise advertising copy will commit wild blunders uncaught by anyone in the agency. An ad for a well-known brand of gin asserts: "The martini has made a return . . . and it's still drank the same way it was sixty years ago." About that, diction hawkshaw Ernest Lorimer comments: "I can understand a liquor company not using the word *drunk* in an ad, but this goes too far." William Safire collects high-pretense illiteracies like these:

> Ad for a costly word processor: "The built-in spelling dictionary instantly alerts you of any spelling errors."

> Ad for an extravagantly expensive wristwatch: "If you are fortunate enough to have an old watch or two laying around . . ." [White House, please take note.]

> And an ad for a . . . Fifth Avenue women's clothing store speaks of "Discrete extravagance."

And it is no longer assumed that writers with showy by-lines on large newspapers will be literate. One of them, writing on a front page about Natan Sharansky, declares that since his flight from the USSR, "there has been time for he and his wife to start a family in Jerusalem." Another, on the front page of the same highly regarded paper: "Mr. Durenberger did not dispute the principle facts in the case." And a few weeks later, in the Sunday travel section: in Cairo "the dominance of pickpockets" is said to be "the principle threat to the traveler's billfold." In 1910, it would be easy to believe that these were mere unfortunate typos. Not now. And although no one expects ads for pizzas and beer to attain very exalted levels of reasoning, the logic of one such teases the mind:

NEW AMSTERDAM

One of the only beers
brewed in New York City.

But of course that is more bad than BAD, being relatively devoid of pretentiousness.

Thus, the results of the widespread American social insecurity, the terror that speaking or writing simply and unfancily will somehow lower the utterer, betraying him or her as a simpleton devoid of class and high style. Multisyllabic ostentation has grown commonplace, but as the critic Northrop Frye once noticed, "the simple is the opposite of the commonplace," and the simple is carefully shunned by those who labor to seem what they would be. That is why they are careful not to say, for example, that cocaine is a popular drug. They say, "Cocaine is the drug of choice." And they imagine we are impressed.

BAD MAGAZINES

You might get the impression that the great consumers of magazines are college boys, with their unshakable loyalty to *Playboy* and *Penthouse, Sports Illustrated, Car and Driver,* and *Muscle & Fitness.* But as buyers of magazines, they are left far behind by the aged, who regularly take in *Modern Maturity* and the *News Bulletin of the American Association of Retired Persons* to a combined total of 38 million copies a month. The old folks, who now have plenty of time to read but who were never great lovers of books, also constitute a substantial number of the 16 million who keep *Reader's Digest* triumphantly afloat, as well as *TV Guide* (16 million) and *National Geographic* (10 million), but the last of these comes so close to being not bad that it can qualify as actually good.

The distance of most of these magazines from bad suggests a special category, one these days almost honorific: *harmless.* Into this we would place also publications which no bright person would want to read but which do no great damage, like the *Soap Opera Digest*, *The Rotarian*, and the *VFW Auxiliary*, all with surprisingly impressive circulations.

Dropping down from there we enter the purlieus of bad, with *People* and *Us* heading the list. Then, descending, the *National Enquirer, American Rifleman*, and down to magazines aimed at the mentally ill, like *Majesty: The Monthly Royal Review*, for people who get an erection when they think of the Queen Mother—or rather of her privileges, furniture, and jewels—and *Soldier of Fortune*, for people who fantasize plunging a trench knife into a foreigner of color, generally smaller than themselves. Below these we find the really bad: *Foreplay, Inside X-Rated Video*, and *Hot Twosomes*, and for the gay community (see *BAD Language*), *Torso, Inches*, and *Uncut*. Bad as these all may be, none is BAD. The reason? None is pretending to be grand.

The BAD magazines are quite different, and they will escape attention unless we know that to find them, we must look not down but up. They are what Tom Wolfe has termed the plutographic publications. He explains: if pornography was "the great vice of the 1970s, plutography— the graphic depiction of the acts of the rich—is the great vice of the 1980s," and it has clearly taken even deeper root in the 1990s. Plutographic magazines are those that try to persuade their snob readers that they are really aristocrats, or at least have, somewhere in or about them, the stuff of aristocracy—invisible as it may be under normal circumstances. Their illusions of special distinction are kept warm by *House & Garden, Architectural Digest, Art and Antiques, Connoisseur* ("We start with the assumption that your time is precious and your taste exquisite"), and *Millionaire* (and doubtless there's some overlap here with readers of *Majesty*). As Wolfe points out, these snob journals are currently flourishing while periodicals of genteel pornography, like *Playboy* and *Penthouse*, are not doing so well. To put it coarsely: sex is out, greed in.

If the function of a bad magazine like *People* is to encourage readers to admire and envy shallow show-business celebrities and various stupid freaks of curious achievements, the function of a BAD magazine like *Connoisseur* is to encourage readers to admire and envy equally shallow people whose premises and persons lend themselves to prettier photography. The objects of admiration and envy in each case are of roughly equal value, but those depicted by *People* at least don't go around pretending that their inherited money has made them wonderful.

BAD MOVIE ACTORS

AND OTHER PLAYERS

Show business is so dependent on illusion, inflation, and fraud that everything connected with it is BAD. Indeed, its main techniques of publicity, misrepresentation, and hyperbole (e.g., "The Greatest Show on Earth") supply a model for BAD everywhere else. The Duke and Dauphin are quite in the American grain.

Almost inevitably BAD are the players America Takes to Its Heart, like Alfred Lunt and Lynn Fontanne and Helen Hayes, undertalented, overpublicized mimes with narrow ranges and little command of voices and styles not their own, which means minimal ability to master a repertory wider and funnier and more instructively tragic than the merely modern American. Provincial players, they can be called, and their limits are so palpable that only rabid publicity can save them. To this category belong many of the male actors of twenty or thirty years ago, like Burgess Meredith, Charlton Heston, Richard Widmark, and Robert Stack. And of course the Gregory Peck who attempted to play Captain Ahab. Inheritors of the tradition are Robert Duvall, Nick Nolte, and Richard Gere, and Bill Cosby, that master of overstatement, as well as Gary Coleman, master mugger at age twenty-three. Bodies like Arnold Schwarzenegger and Sylvester Stallone belong in a class by themselves, exemplars of Don Lessem's Law, "The louder and less talented you are, the more famous you will become." Tom Hanks, Helen Slater, George Hamilton, Peter Falk, Robert Mitchum, Roseanne Barr, Ricardo Montalban, Charles Bronson, Omar Sharif, Burt Reynolds, Patrick Swayze—none of those should be overlooked, nor Linda Darnell forgotten. All have a nice line in mugging and shouting, underlining each emotion lest the audience not get it.

Some players are so limited that they can project only their own personalities, like Barbra Streisand and Carol Burnett. This is notably true of one of the classic BAD actors of all time, Ronald Reagan, slick in his movie parts, disastrous in his attempt to play "President." And then there are the fatties like Orson Welles and Marlon Brando, once svelte and able, but finally so victimized by the good life as defined by American acquisitiveness and hedonism as to be unpresentable except when shown sitting down in virtual darkness. For American BAD actors, character rapidly becomes caricature. One caricature actress, Margaret Hamilton, the wicked witch of *The Wizard of Ox*, went on hamming and mugging and shrieking in repertory and summer stock until her eighties, causing reviewer John Simon to comment on one of her performances, wonderfully if cruelly, "Margaret Hamilton is eighty-two but looks older."

To get a sense of how very BAD American actors are, try to imagine Ernest Borgnine playing Dogberry, Hume Cronyn Oedipus, Don Ameche King Lear, Sally Field Lady Macbeth, or Tom Cruise Iago. What international embarrassment would ensue if Paul Newman, talented as he is, tried to persuade us that he is Benedick, or Anthony Quinn that he is Tartuffe. Dustin Hoffman may not be perfect, but at least now and then he manifests the real actor's urge to pretend to be Shylock or Willie Loman.

As if stage and screen didn't keep us in ample supply, scores of BAD actors are to be found on the podium, writhing and posturing and overplaying and faking in front of symphony orchestras. Acting must be very difficult, it must be admitted, when your audience is behind you and your means are restricted to your hands and the back of your head and the back of your tails, and the dramatistic excesses of conductors may be attributed to their natural urge to overcome these limits on expression. One who worked very hard overcoming these restrictions was Leonard Bernstein, who made himself almost the definitive figure here and virtual world champion of BAD "maestro" enactment. Donal Henahan is one of many music critics who had Bernstein's number. Bernstein's touching vanity prompted him to conduct programs of the "B" composers, like Beethoven and Brahms, so that he could include, as if by alliterative obligation, compositions by guess who. Vulgar audiences, Donal Henahan notes, adored Bernstein's "obvious involvement with the music and his actor's skill in miming its meaning so vividly that a deaf person might easily enjoy his concerts." But Bernstein often went Too Far, and ended by managing to "steal the show from the music." Henahan wearied of watching him perform one easy stunt, witnessed during Brahms's Fourth Symphony, where "he let his arms hang limply and conducted with henlike nods of the head and expressive shoulder shrugs, . . . an old trick of European conductors" and one which forces the audience to attend to "the oddly unemployed conductor at the expense of the music itself." And Bernstein seemed quite incorrigible because, as

Henahan observes, "no conductor of our time enjoys such wonderful rapport with himself as Mr. Bernstein."

Once, orchestral conductors were anonymous time-beaters. Wagner's performances of Beethoven changed all that and helped establish the BAD modern tradition that the conductor is as grand as the conducted. As one critic notes, the Rumanian Sergiu Celibidache is famous for "his elaborate care on stage to share applause with his players." Celibidache is doubtless an impressive musical intelligence, but "egotism such as [his] usurps creative power from that which it proposes to serve." Leopold Stokowski was another in this egotistic line, and Charles Münch took himself terribly seriously, convinced that it was he, not the orchestra, and certainly not the music, that was "the hearth to which thousands have come for warmth and light."

Elaborate and unremitting publicity is required to sustain the reputations for sensitivity and profundity of a number of current BAD favorites. Zubin Mehta—"a flashy conductor with no depth," one expert calls him—may be said to head the list, closely followed by the superficial Seiji Ozawa, whose photographic memory allows him to grasp a score instantly—and without study. It is said that the players of the Boston Symphony once almost rebelled under Ozawa's leadership, asserting that they "learned nothing from him." Way down the BAD list you would find Leonard Slatkin, and farther down still, Sir Neville Marriner, who, failing to impress judicious listeners to the Minnesota Orchestra, now conducts a successful show business in London, recording with, apparently, minimal rehearsals everything in sight. Like BAD actors, BAD conductors know that the audience is too dull and uninstructed to catch them out or in any way grow suspicious of the kudos generated by public relations counselors (formerly press agents).

What do unemployed symphony conductors do? One

can guess that they teach violin in small, seedy conservatories somewhere or give courses in music appreciation at the least impressive American learneries (see *BAD Colleges and Universities*). There is less mystery about the destiny of unemployed actors. Most of the bad ones, who've not had enough jobs and exposure to graduate to BAD, function as waiters and waitresses. For them, see *BAD Restaurants*.

BAD MOVIES

Who can remember, before BAD movies, when bad movies were simply bad? When they were attractions like *Robot vs. the Aztec Mummy* or *Santa Claus Conquers the Martians*? In those days, when it was movie-theater demand alone that turned popcorn into a gold-mine farm commodity, it wasn't hard to spot a bad movie well in advance. A "desert island" or "jungle" motif could usually be counted on to promise clinkers like *Island of Desire,* with Linda Darnell and Tab Hunter, *Blue Lagoon* ("a total fraud from beginning to end"—*Guardian*), or *Out of Africa,* starring Robert Redford and Meryl Streep. In the same way, well before the days of Sylvester Stallone and Arnold Schwarzenegger (see *BAD Movie Actors and Other Players*) beefcake was a tip-off that your money and time would be better spent elsewhere. All you had to be vouchsafed was a title like *Hercules in the Vale of Woe* to know that you should head for the nearest saloon instead. Another warning signal used to be any hint of a biblical or religious theme, as in *The Robe* or (rock bottom) *The Bible*. Most "war movies" were also bad, and experienced ex-soldiers were especially contemptuous of those in which artillery and mortar shells went *whooosssh* when they went off with big showy gouts of oil-produced flame instead of the authentic (but nonvisual) deafening *crack!* Likewise, before 1970 or thereabouts, it was fairly certain that any movie with a would-be sexy title was going to be bad. The brighter moviegoers learned to read a rip-off from a distance by noticing words in movie titles like *night, paradise, French* (especially lubricious, that one), *desire, flesh,* or *sex* (cf. *Sex Kittens Go to College*—see *BAD Colleges and Universities*).

Because of the contemporary phenomenon of accelerating Prole Drift (analyzed in my book *Class*), among the intelligent the threat of a remake was almost always a cause of sinking spirits as viewers experienced repeated disappointments comparing the 1964 *Night Must Fall* with the good one of 1937, the 1962 *Mutiny on the Bounty* with the original of 1935, the 1959 *Tarzan, the Ape Man* with the Johnny Weissmuller prototype of 1932, or the 1950 Disney version of *Treasure Island*—great obtrusive *pizzicato* passages in the background music used, like the TV laugh track, to cue the audience how to react—with the good one of 1934, which gave such grand curiosities as Lionel Barrymore and Wallace Beery the chance to character-act. (The one exception to the bad remake axiom is the 1978 version of *Invasion of the Body Snatchers,* a rethinking by Don Siegel of the sad 1956 effort and redeemed also by the old-style subtlety and respect for the audience of Donald Sutherland's acting and Philip Kaufman's directing.) Despite the obvious folly of trying to remake *Modern Times, Citizen Kane, Casablanca, High Noon,* or even *On the Waterfront* or *Hud,* someone (see *BAD People*) is sure to try and then, when the contempt pours in, respond by designating the critics *elitist*.

•

That used to be the scene, but now BAD has taken over, which means that this is the age of the blockbuster, the cartoonish *Star Wars* and its sequels, *Superman* and its sequels, *E. T., Batman,* and *Dick Tracy,* movies in which, as Todd Gitlin has said, "the sum of the publicity takes up more cultural space than the movie itself." With the super-hype, there's room in the public mind for only one movie at a time, and it must be the right one, publicized so that no one in the United States (and usually Europe and Asia as well), regardless of his or her habits of attention or scorn for advertising, can be unaware of it. The favored time to release a blockbuster is June: the adolescents who are its audience are newly sprung from school and ready to rush their saved-up money to the box office. But the hype begins well back near the beginning of the spring semester. That's when the first planted publicity stories start to bloom, the first bales of T-shirts begin swelling the wholesalers' warehouses, the first dolls and novelties appear in the malls. By June, the kids are drooling like Pavlov's dogs, and the success of the newest BAD movie is virtually guaranteed, no matter how bad it proves. (I say "virtually" because now and then the system fails. Michael Cimino's *Heaven's Gate* was supposed to be this kind of infantile blockbuster. It cost $44 million, but turned out "totally incoherent," in the words of one critic, and as Vince Staten says, it is "generally credited with bankrupting United Artists." [Aside: There *is* a God!] Actually, *Apocalypse Now* was just as BAD, but somehow few people found out.)

The blockbuster embodies the whole idea of BAD because it is empty of human value at the heart and depends entirely on overstatement, succeeding only because supported by publicity. Instead of adult narrative and acting, it offers comic-strip motivations and an almost exclusive reliance on special effects, gratifying to the uneducated (see *BAD Colleges and Universities*) who have never learned to achieve excitement over anything but technology. (It is for these that the whole NASA dramaturgy is enacted: they think it interesting and significant.) As Peter Biskind has said, the object of the blockbuster is—should civilized adults actually see one—"to reconstitute the audience as children." The obvious effect, in the absence of the counterweight of education, has been "the infantilization of the electorate," resulting in, among other things, the election of Ronald Reagan and George Bush and the agitation over flag desecration. And the blockbuster is by no means a thing in itself. It is rather, as Mark Miller emphasizes, a merchandising tool to move other (Time Warner) commodities, like Batman "shoes and shorts, hats and place mats . . . a Time Warner rock video . . . several paperbacks from Warner Books . . . a cover story in *Time* magazine," and the like. The movie, says Miller, is now simply a "cog, or chip, within a mammoth image-generating system that includes TV production companies and syndication firms, cable distribution networks, record companies, theme parks . . . as well as publishing companies, major magazines, and many newspapers."

Little wonder, then, that the movie blockbusters are as empty of grown-up content as that other typical and expressive American invention, light beer. The only thing they offer more of than TV dramas, perforce censored for family viewing, is violence, with chain-saw massacres and kickings in the crotch constituting what you can see nowhere else and exactly what you go to movies to see. Where you used to go to watch Cary Grant and Irene Dunne, fully clothed, playing out their subtle flirtations in the witty mode of indoor social theater, now you watch rapes, beatings, the lopping off of limbs, faces ruined and bleeding, eyes hanging out on cheeks, blood spurting from arteries, sharks devouring children—the whole sadistic stagecraft of the Jacobean drama or of Grand Guignol. Everything demeans the audience, and the sole technique is overemphasis (see *BAD Conversation, BAD Music*). As Mark Miller says, today's movies, blockbuster or run-of-the-mill, go in for "that systematic overemphasis deployed in advertising (and all other propaganda). Each shot presents a content closed and unified, like a fist, and makes the point right in your face: big gun, big car, nice ass, full moon . . . big crash (blood, glass). . . ." And after this violent trash is finally over, there will be an interminable run-through of credits, just as if something worth taking credit for had been achieved. Then we learn the names of everyone remotely connected with the BAD movie, together with their relatives and sex objects:

> Third Assistant Grip:
> Third Assistant Grip's Assistant:
> Gaffer:
> Gaffer's Assistant:
> Gaffer's Assistant's Girlfriend:

There's an analogue in *BAD Books* (q.v.), whose pretentious prefaces and acknowledgments thank whole regiments of benefactors—with names as famous as possible—as if to spread the blame.

BAD MUSIC

Music, any music at all, is so welcome to the weak of mind and so readily supplied by their commercial manipulators that almost all the music you hear, at least all you hear inadvertently, is bad. It grows BAD as, like other things, it becomes pretentious and, because it is thought to be Art, asks to be treated respectfully. And here, distinctions like "classical" and "popular" are close to meaningless. Much of the Beatles' and Simon and Garfunkel's music is better written than most of the music of Sir Edward Elgar, and only outright snobbery could find great difference between the banal repetitiveness of Percy Grainger's *Country Gardens* and the latest reggae hit, although for insensitive overstatement and pure unvarying noise, the reggae would probably win the prize. Both depend on such BAD techniques as repetition without development and a lack of closure (see *BAD Signs*) and thus resemble *BAD Conversation* (q.v.).

Thus, in music, boring is BAD, whether the music

takes place in a concert hall or a bawdy house and whether it's played by a string quartet or a steel band. There are certain trustworthy signs that BAD is either present or in the offing—like flagrant harp arpeggios (check those flying fingers!), or, in piano playing, the Liberace trick of raising the hands as high as possible above the keyboard to exhibit energy and athleticism, the motive also of the most kinetic symphony conductors (see *BAD Movie Actors and Other Players*). More clues to the presence of BAD are musical clichés that beg for attention and admiration and assume that the audience is so stupid that it has not heard them a thousand times before. In banality, these are the equivalent of the climactic passages on the Wurlitzer that orchestrate emotion at baseball and basketball games and cue the audience to shout in unison, "Charge!" And you can be fairly certain that compositions aspiring to transport you to exotic, usually Eastern, locales ("Song of India"; "In a Chinese Temple Garden") will range from BAD to VERY BAD. By the same token, anything labeled "Nocturne" should be approached gingerly. And critic Jack Lynch suggests that the BAD prize be awarded to "any piece of music ever written, played, sung, performed, produced, funded, encouraged, criticized, or heard by Andrew Lloyd Webber."

But the handiest rule of thumb is that a piece of music that doesn't Get Anywhere (like most reggae) is bad. A piece that doesn't Get Anywhere while pretending to be rare and valuable, and even spiritual, like the *Pachelbel Kanon in D,* is BAD. As BAD as music that pretends to Get Somewhere by mechanical means like facile modulation upward to burnish and disguise each repetition, or mere intensification of tempo and volume. Easier than invention. (Example: Ravel's *Bolero,* or Music to Copulate By.) In music these devices are the equivalent of similar frauds in the theater, like the time-honored stage manager's trick of slyly advancing the rheostat and brightening the lights to suggest an increase of enthusiasm with each curtain call.

There is one handy gauge of both bad and BAD: the music piped to you in all but the most sophisticated banks, bookstores, and elevators, and the music forced upon you on the phone while you wait, and wait, for your tardy, BAD interlocutor. It is significant that these musics are seldom by Byrd, Purcell, Telemann, Handel, or Rameau, and seldom even by Mozart, although the vulgarities of *Amadeus* (almost as popular among *BAD People* [q.v.] as *Equus*) have made it modish among businessmen and similar philistines to affect a fondness for Mozart. By playing to your phone delayees the *Pachelbel Kanon* you can get high marks for sincerity, if not outright piety.

In his valuable book *The Worst of Everything*, Don Lessem has performed a public service by naming the Most Boring Pieces of Music ("Music to Snore By"). The list of course includes *Bolero* and Dvořák's *New World Symphony*. Vivaldi's *Four Seasons* is there also, and so are Anton Bruckner's *Symphony No. 9 in D Minor* and Charles Ives's *Three Places in New England*. Acute as he is, Lessem has somehow overlooked the works of John Cage, although he has noticed that there's something excessively uninteresting about the music of Philip Glass. Lessem thinks Tchaikovsky's *Fifth Symphony* notably tedious, but in my view it can't at all come up to Sibelius's *Finlandia*. Others might want to nominate the less brisk passages in *Der Ring des Nibelungen*, or the whole of *Tosca*, grace notes included.

BAD Movies (q.v.) have persuaded many young couples to get married to the strains of themes from blockbusters like *Star Wars* or *Chariots of Fire*, suggesting the almost magical power of BAD in one place to trigger BAD in another.

BAD NAVAL

MISSILE FIRING

Q. Who caused the crash of the Pan Am 747 at Lockerbie, Scotland?

A. The United States Navy.

Q. How?

A. The Pan Am plane was destroyed to avenge the BAD missile firing by the Navy that brought down an Iranian airliner some months before. The Navy's mistake—it thought the civilian plane a fighter plane about to attack—was in large part occasioned by reliance on grandiose electronic sensing and aiming equipment. It was also caused by the sailors' being scared so shitless— or so automatically following Navy regulations—that they wouldn't allow the terrifying object to get close enough to be identified by an old-fashioned CPO looking at it through binoculars.

Q. Was this sort of reliance on showy technology also responsible for the turret explosion on the USS *Iowa,* as well as the various U.S. Navy collisions and runnings-aground that followed, so embarrassing that naval activity ceased for a while so that officers could try to figure out what was wrong?

A. Very likely. What was wrong was BAD.

BAD NEWSPAPERS

Admittedly, a *Le Monde* we have not got—part of the cost of separating the seat of government from the seat of wit and intelligence and contriving that hundreds-of-miles stretch between Pennsylvania Avenue and Wall Street. But we do have three or four good newspapers, and we have hundreds of bad ones, identifiable by one or more of the following stigmata.

By their features ye shall know them: comic strips, of course, and daily horoscopes, and a great vacancy where a civilized reader might expect a book review. Weekly summaries of the TV soap-opera plots. Daily prayers, often right on the front page. An Inquiring Photographer (more accurately, Fotographer) feature, solemnly delivering the opinions of the dumb and the ignorant, and a letters-to-the-editor column offering readers' silly views on the most inflammatory-trivial local topics. In addition to these indicators, here as elsewhere the lavish use of color will reveal that you are in a journalistic atmosphere on the psychological level of a grade school, with the world as a Sunday funny paper. There was a time when the only color visible on a newspaper page was that of Old Glory at the top of Hearst's front pages, an earnest against bolshevism and foreign ideas in general. Now, a paper without a large color photo on the front page—above the fold, of course—risks losing appeal among the untutored, who demand literal representationalism ("realism") everywhere, with a concomitant inability to appreciate irony or metaphor—unless it takes the form of cliché. One bright paper on the West Coast implicitly comments on the intellectual condition of readers who like colored pictures. It confines them to the sports pages.

Bad papers employ and actually pay writers who don't know how to compose a lead paragraph, and who make you read 250 words before you find out what the subject of the obituary died of or where the shooting took place. Bad newspapers also work as many puns as possible into their headlines. On a story about deer eating backyard shrubs, for example:

DEER NIBBLING AWAY AT ONCE-DEAR IMAGE

Bad papers specialize in using a certain number of "stars" to indicate a critic's view of the quality of a movie or restaurant, without bothering to tell you what they mean. In bad papers the writing becomes the flashy, pseudo-intimate sort demanded by a near-illiterate audience corrupted further by show business and thus incapable of dealing with prose that is in any way complicated, subtle, allusive, ironic, outrageous, unexpected, or really funny. Mencken! thou shouldst be living at this hour: America hath need of thee, etc.

Almost all these characteristics are conspicuous in the one newspaper that has had the impudence to designate itself The Nation's Newspaper. (Actually the *Wall Street Journal* is, but let that pass.) *USA Today* is a remarkably pure model of the BAD principle: it is empty at the center but has a technically showy surface. It represents an exemplary triumph of presentation over substance. A test of this newspaper's right to the name might include questions like: what is its position on a given issue? who cares what it thinks? who wants to write for it, and what is his or her quality? who wants to read it, and what is he or she like? The idea of a mind nourished only on TV and *USA Today* is not one to console anyone nervous about an intelligent future, but that mind is precisely the one that supports—nay, celebrates—BAD everywhere.

USA Today, which first appeared in 1982 with the installation of Ronald Reagan as the favorite American, is the perfect emblem of Reaganism. Its founder, Al Neuharth, conceived it, he said, as a weapon against "the old journalism of despair," which, he felt, left readers discouraged or indignant. "A new journalism of hope" was to be promulgated by *USA Today*, perfectly in keeping with a wider American cosmeticizing, from the leader's hair dye to the concealment of aid to the Contras. It's no surprise that *USA Today* was one of the commercial "sponsors" of Ronald Reagan's second inauguration.

It is the relentless pursuit of the upbeat that provides the half-adolescent, half-Babbitty tone of the paper. One of its headlines about an airline crash has become famous:

MIRACLE: 327 SURVIVE, 55 DIE.

What really gave Neuharth the idea that a whole new kind of journalism might find favor was the success of superficiality, color, and populist simplification on television, especially on its news shows (see *BAD Television*). (Hoping recently to validate and recommend Dan Rather, *USA To-*

day quoted one of his colleagues designating him "a regular guy," fond of baseball and hunting and fishing and enjoying a good chaw when out in the woods. Conclusion: who wants distinction anyway?) To entice an audience already hooked on TV, Neuharth finally settled, after prolonged experimentation, on a sidewalk dispensing stand bearing as close a resemblance as possible to a TV set on a pedestal, with the top half of the newspaper aping the TV screen. Television's way with the news provides a model for *USA Today*'s editorial procedures, and not merely its ostentatious use of graphics, most of them merely showy and unnecessary. Like TV news departments, Neuharth's paper has few reporters but lots of editors, rewriters, presenters, fixers-up, suppliers of the proper company tone, and similar executants of the egotistic publisher's will. The central news-preparation room is full of overhead TV sets, as if to encourage the kept wordsmiths to adjust their emissions to accord with the TV's. One critic noted when the paper first appeared, "Television fans can now have their tube and read it too." And it's certainly the entertainment industry that determines the prevailing concerns and idiom of *USA Today*. Everything possible connected even remotely with show business receives major attention and display, and even accounts of phenomena distant from "entertainment" assume an audience lost without some connection with TV and BAD-movie culture. For example, a story about the Supreme Court's return to the flag-destruction issue begins, "Call it flag-burning, The Sequel."

The special verbal techniques of *USA Today* are so unremittingly in evidence that it's easy to see the way it has raised normal journalistic bad to BAD. Neuharth commanded his writers and toadies to use the word *America* as little as possible and to replace it with *USA,* which can thus function as constant advertising and promotion. The assumption that the paper's dumb readers can't stand actuality unless it's "treated" and transformed into entertainment results in the usual would-be clever headlines, relying on irrelevant rhymes,

WHAT'S HOT IN TRUNKS FOR HUNKS,

alliteration,

PARTISAN POTSHOTS PREVIEW TAX TALKS,

and puns:

FLAG STARS AGAIN BEFORE HIGH COURT

[ROLLER] COASTERS CLIMB TO NEW HEIGHTS

[News of a flagrantly expensive tour:]
WORLD IS YOUR OYSTER FOR 39,500 CLAMS

But curiously, there are few such high jinks in the sports section (one-fourth of the paper), where it might be supposed they belong. The implication: sports are too serious for joking, even if the rest of the paper gives the impression that Life Is a Cabaret, and that despite such embarrassments as two world wars, a Holocaust, a Vietnam War, and a gulf one (to mention just a few), everything is just fine, and we should keep on the way we're going ("Stay the course."—Ronald Reagan) to create a wonderful world where there will be wonderful things for people to buy and enjoy. A standard warning to university freshmen embarking on the composition course is never to call attention to your clichés by enclosing them in quotation marks. *USA Today* rejects that elitist advice and makes its readers comfortable by doing it their way:

SAGGING HOME [!] SALES PUT 'ON HOLD'

ON NBC, A 'QUANTUM LEAP' OF FAITH

And who are the readers of this stuff, whose devotion to *USA Today* has brought its circulation into dangerous competition with the *New York Times* and the *Wall Street Journal*? Their identity can be inferred from a glance at the advertisers convinced that in taking out a lot of expensive space they will be reaching the very audience they have in mind. In one recent issue, appearing in the midst of the dispute about continuing the appropriation for the National Endowment for the Arts, the Reverend Pat Robertson's "Christian Coalition" thought its money well spent on a full-page ad featuring these questions, addressed to members of Congress (presumed, notice, to be readers of this paper):

> Do you . . . want to face the voters with the charge that you are wasting their hard-earned money to promote sodomy, child pornography, and attacks on Jesus Christ?

And, Mr. Congressman, do you think that "decent working people" want their tax money spent "to teach their sons how to sodomize one another"? In the same issue, the American Legion and thirteen similar organizations unite to finance a half-page ad addressed to the same audience anxious about their boys' susceptibility to the attractions of buggery:

FLAG BURNING: IN YOUR HEART YOU KNOW IT'S WRONG.

(An unacknowledged steal of the Republican sign on behalf, once, of Barry Goldwater: "In Your Heart You Know

He's Right," to which opponents attached an immensely successful extension: "Yes, Far Right." The inserters of this anti-flag-burning ad assume, doubtless correctly, that the public they're addressing is too stupid as well as humorless to know or to remember that.) If ads like those don't provide a sufficient clue to the readership, then the numerous ads promoting cars, motorcycles, and durable goods like refrigerators and gimmick garage doors will suggest a heavily macho audience. (The words *Via Satellite* at the top of *USA Today*'s front pages are designed to impress such technology-fascinated readers, easily imagined also as fans of *Popular Mechanics* and *Home Office Computing*.) And not just macho: gullible as well, as a brief browse among the classified ads will indicate. Those who advertise there know their audience thoroughly and have had long experience of its suckerhood, which can be exploited by such rube come-ons as

MAKE BIG $$$

or

BE RICH AND FAMOUS

Many of the *USA Today* classified ads seek to entice readers into commission schemes selling products of very doubtful appeal, like a new line of diet brownies or an amazing stain remover "as seen on TV." You can also generate high commissions by selling a new "Life Extension Secret" or the "Hottest Thing Going in the 90s: Non-Surgical Face Lift. Be the first agent in your area. Great Profit Potential." There is an injunction to "Start Your Own Travel Agency," an almost surefire formula for financial heartache, second only to "Start Your Own Restaurant" or "Make Big Money Writing Children's Books." Other ads offer for sale numerous failed motels and similar unpromising commercial premises: "BECOME RICH!" Thank God it's the social welfare agencies and psychiatric institutions, not we, and certainly not *USA Today,* that have to deal, finally, with the ruined victims of these presentations. And it's a sobering thought that, according to a Simmons Market Research survey of *USA Today* readers, 68 percent have "attended college," and are thus "well-educated people" (see *BAD Colleges and Universities*).

An unpleasant fact (in the present instance) is that people become what they read. Even the *Official Boy Scout Handbook* knows this, and it knows the consequences and has the courage to specify them: "Reading trash all the time," it declares unequivocally, "makes it impossible for anyone to be anything but a second-rate person." A good reason to encourage the sprouts who've not yet been degraded and demeaned to beware of BAD newspapers. The plural there and in the heading of this section might be held to mislead if it weren't certain that very soon there will be more newspapers in the mode of *USA Today.* Its success practically guarantees a plethora of successors, all BAD.

BAD OBJECTS,
WITH AN EXCURSUS
ON COLLECTIBLES

Some objects are so obviously BAD that they are immediately embraced by the middle class, while objects that are merely bad (e.g., plaster Popeyes atop TV sets) gladden the hearts of the classes below. To lust after objects that are BAD, you have to think yourself rather special and desirable. One object that occasions a flutter among people like that is the "Greek fisherman's cap." This is favored by aging middle-class men aspiring to an appearance of youth, sophistication, and rakishness. If frank proletarians favor the plastic visor cap with words like *Old Fart* on the front and the handy adjusto-strap in the rear, the Greek fisherman's get-up is the prole cap of those who sway to the urgings of the *New Yorker* and its ads. Roy Blount, Jr., has nicely stigmatized the bogosity of wearing this BAD object:

No one ought to wear a Greek fisherman's cap who doesn't meet two qualifications:
1. He is Greek.
2. He is a fisherman.

But then any hat worn by men risks BADness, especially
headgear aspiring to escape the ordinary, like oversized
berets that hang down on all sides, snoods, or the squarish
tams worn by those academics who conceive that the mortarboard has seen its day (see *BAD Colleges and Universities*).
Workmen can wear hard hats on construction sites without
blame, but when mayors, governors, or presidents affect
them during a rapid visit, the effect is BAD.

All objects give off artistic, social, and moral overtones, and every object one associates with is likely to betray one's badness or BADness. Among the Rich and
Famous there are dreadful types who buy the most awful
objects distinguished by nothing but exhibitionistic prices.
Indeed, the more you know about the R and F, the less
occasion there will be for envy. Diamonds are bad enough,
ostentatious and pretentious, appropriate only to be flourished by show-off trash like Diamond Lil and Diamond
Jim Brady. But to go them one further, you can now have
the diamonds on your rings or necklace or wristwatch dis-
played in "freely moving settings," so that when you move,
the jewels will flop around on little hinges, maximizing the
glitter and presumably impressing moronic onlookers.
This innovation, exciting to women who wear spike heels
with their Levi's and affect swimsuits of gold lamé, is said
to have been devised by a watch manufacturer in Geneva,
and his ads indicate his pride in thus achieving BAD in a
new way, or, as he puts it, in his "unique concept":

> Ten years ago _____ designed the first pat-
> ented watch with freely moving diamonds. Based on
> this original idea an entire collection of watches and
> jewelry is now available.

(Note, by the way, the ambiguous participle *based on*, much
favored by *BAD People* [q.v.] who also say *plus* when they
mean *and*; as well as the bogus term *collection*, used by

dishonorable merchandisers hoping to depict their vulgar truck as "works of art" [see *BAD Advertising*].)

Indeed, jewelry "firsts" are inevitably BAD, and most emanate—or so the pretense is—from Geneva. Another watch company there advertises "An historic first [note the snob pseudo-British *an* instead of *a*] in the history of watch-making":

> ———— proudly introduces the specially numbered
> Tourbillon Minute Repeater with Perpetual Calendar
> in a Skeleton Automatic,

skeleton meaning, apparently, see-through. If you slaver for real BAD, that watch will cost you $250,000—a lot of money, to be sure, but think how impressed your audience will be. BAD watches like that always deliver information you don't want: month, week, and day, phases of the moon, astrological sign, "perpetual calendar," and so on. If a quarter of a million is a bit high for you, or if you frequent a society not quite so BAD as the one this jeweler imagines, you can get a trimmed-down version of this kind of see-through watch at Tiffany's (shows moon phases, etc.) for $21,500.

Clearly aimed at a similarly BAD, if not so publicly rich, audience is "personalized 14-Karat Gold Name Jewelry," with emphasis on your first name, lest you forget it or lest others, who might be tempted to call you "Mr. Something," ignore their duty as friendly Americans to be as informal as possible. Your Name in Gold ("hand cut") occupies the center of "His" gold bracelet or "Her" gold necklace or bracelet. Each constitutes "your very own personal fashion statement" (see *BAD Advertising*).

Because you are allowed only eight letters, the depicted sample of the woman's bracelet, designed for "Katherine," has had rudely to compress her name to an

illiterate and vulgar "Kathryn," making the item even
more Hollywood and BAD. "Sleek sophistication" is the
effect you will achieve, the ad for these things promises;
and they are of course *presented* (see *BAD Language*) in
their own jeweler's gift *cases* (formerly, *boxes*). If some scru-
ple of decency, modesty, or taste inhibits you from advertising your whole name, you can compromise with a ring
depicting your script initial in—what else?—diamonds.
"The result," says the ad, "is a look that's different," a
point no one will gainsay. Nor will surprise be occasioned
by diction which nicely accords with the whole idea: "The
handsome Man's Diamond Initial Ring can be ordered for
the ring finger or as a *pinky* ring." A man who treasures
one of these is clearly also a prospect for the injector razor
with a genuine Waterford crystal handle "superbly pat-
terned with wedge and diamond cuts." Presented in a
"satin-lined gift box," this provides "the most elegant way
a man can shave." The problem, however, is that no one
will be able to admire your BAD object unless you invite
your guests into your bathroom on some pretext or other
to watch you shave.

That's a small BAD object. There are many large ones.
The stretch limousine, for example: it has become so common now that it's easy to ignore how BAD it is, even if it
remains black instead of white (see *BAD Behavior*). The
more it is designed to cause the mouths of the untutored
to drop open, the more BAD it is. There's a man in New
York named Tedd (get that BAD spelling) Abramson who
has created (as he would say) the longest white stretch limo
allowed by law. The ordinary one is twenty-three feet long.
His runs to thirty-five feet. Journalist Mark Seal indicates
what is likely to happen when this BAD spectacle appears:

> Rounding the corner of West 46th Street onto Broad-
> way, the longest limousine in New York City nearly

causes a riot. Diners hop from their booths to crowd the restaurant windows. Wild-eyed bums and screaming street kids race along the boulevard. Beautiful women trot over from the George M. Cohan statue to check out the commotion. Tourists try to guess who's inside. Trump? . . . Carson? Eddie Murphy? . . . Eyes bulge, jaws drop. A hundred index fingers point, and a dozen cameras click.

This object of intense interest and desire is a Lincoln Town Car with six wheels, "three moon roofs, 10 tinted windows . . . three telephones, two TVs, a VCR, a stereo, and three bed-like burgundy glove-leather [see *BAD Advertising*] couches . . . and a Jacuzzi in the back." (Using the Jacuzzi will cost you $500 extra.) The bar is paneled in ebony, "the same wood Donald Trump used in his limousine," says Tedd. And is this monster unique? No. "Already there are similar limousines in California," Mr. Seal assures us. You can rent Tedd's ultimate limo for $160 an hour (four-hour minimum), and if you do so, it would be a crime against BAD not to inform your guests how much it costs. Tedd, not surprisingly, dreams of "owning a fleet of block-long limousines and a summer home [see *BAD Language*] in Hawaii."

But at least the stretch limo, no matter how long, avoids the mark of many BAD objects, the stigma of the *ersatz*. In Southern California and similar places, what is called "cultured stone" is popular for the insides and outsides of "homes." This consists of phony rocks with rounded surfaces, made from real rock that has been pulverized and then reconstituted—a sort of stone plastic, as it were. These BAD objects come with one flat side so you can deceive your audience by appliquéing them onto your walls, fireplaces, etc., with adhesive. This *ersatz* material has a counterpart in "bonded marble," favored for the mass reproduction of well-known classical and Renaissance sculptures. Carving marble is costly and requires talent. Molding powdered marble together with a binder is cheap and easy. A little Michelangelo *David* can thus easily be turned out in versions ranging from twelve to forty-eight inches high, as opposed to the sixteen and a half feet of the original. "What a piece of work is a man!" exclaims an ad for this BAD object, hoping that the judicious won't notice that this parodic reduction of the original to mini-size demeans both the man represented and the man who carved him. But then demeaning comes naturally once you've learned to relish the cheap and easy and nasty, while pretending to celebrate the grand and traditional.

BAD in a similar way is the new item in men's evening dress—i.e., "white tie." With tails, you used to wear a white piqué vest. Now increasingly you see people wearing not that vest but a vile satin, or more likely acrylic mock-satin, white cummerbund, in apparent imitation of the colored ones rented by high school boys to add dash to their prom wear. Some *ersatz* objects go even further toward BAD, like the wallpaper you can buy for your "study" depicting shelves of books, their titles judiciously soft-focused. This, a decorator notes, is "a wallpaper for those who like the library look but don't want to be bothered with books." In the demeaning department also are those canes relied on by the elderly and the handicapped made of metal instead of wood. With a little taste and a refusal to be enticed into the BAD-object game, such people could just as well carry nice wooden, even antique, walking sticks, perhaps even with some nonstandard, charming, or eccentric design or carving. Thus they could celebrate and participate in two class and value principles at once—the principle that things made of organic materials are nicer than those that are not, and the principle that the archaic form of anything traditional is to be preferred. But these poor victims of *ersatz* must carry their metal canes—prescribed, presumably, by physicians without taste—just as if they were appropriate and even beautiful.

Other BAD objects escape the stigma of the *ersatz* but succumb to temptations of grandeur, or self-defeating fanciness. Take that classic BAD object; the chrome-plated, two-levered "butterfly" corkscrew, much favored by the middle class, which has never profited from noticing the way a French waiter calmly and effectively pulls a cork without breaking it or pinching his fingers, and without involving himself with a mechanism containing the maximum number of moving parts, all of which can be counted on ultimately to go wrong. The screw fixture on this showy BAD American corkscrew usually wears out within a year, but the corkscrew is kept around and employed forever, working worse each time it's used. (And see *BAD Engineering.*)

You'd have to be quite thick not to notice the way the mere idea of *wine* generates insatiable desires for BAD in consumers and avidity to gratify them in manufacturers and suppliers. Wine writer Frank Prial has called attention to the $4,000 wine refrigerator with wood panels, glass doors, and interior lights. It will show everyone that you know enough to keep your white wine cold, and as Prial says, it will "make [your] dining room look like an all-night convenience store." And there's that quintessential BAD object the wine-bottle basket, which can suggest to the naïve that the bottle it encradles contains a vintage so precious that standing the bottle erect would be an act adjacent to sacrilege. There's the BAD object mentioned by Prial "that pumps nitrogen into your unfinished bottle of wine, preserving it, if not for posterity, at least until you get around to drinking it a day or two hence." Of this, he says, "I don't know. There never seems to be any wine left over *chez moi.* Am I doing something wrong?" The acute observer will notice how often these BAD wine objects will be found in households where the glasses, referred to as "crystal," are made of colored glass showily cut and patterned. In such houses, it's a fair bet that you can find a chess set designed for people who go in as little for chess as, actually, for wine.

It would indeed be hard to find objects so precisely illustrating the most rigorous definition of BAD as fancy chess sets. As if Nathaniel Cook and Howard Staunton didn't know what they were doing designing the standard chess pieces in the mid-nineteenth century, these BAD chess sets feature pieces which come on as cute characters in *Alice in Wonderland,* say, or as men and women of the Raj in India, or as the people in such folk narratives as "The Emperor's New Clothes," or as tiny reproductions of the troops engaged in the Civil War. Wot larks! Here, the pawns are infantrymen, Union and Confederate, respectively, the knights are cavalrymen, and the two kings are Generals Grant and Lee, their "queens" represented by a Northern "lady" and a Southern "belle." Playing with these pieces, it may be true, as the ad has it, that "chess becomes a battle between battalions of 'the blue and the grey,' " but it certainly ceases to be chess. But no matter: chess is not in the minds of those who acquire these sets: BADness is, and the lust for a reputation as a judicious thinker is almost as easily gratified by chess sets whose impossible pieces are bits of pointed and polished rock or sharpened bits of wood.

As has surely become clear already, most common, unpretentious objects that someone has tried to "improve" or impose novelty upon turn out to be BAD, and sometimes very BAD. How about those "wallets" worn in front at stomach level, which make all look like vendors or front-heavy freaks, and which make the obese look even fatter? Or how about a man's "attention-getting, satin-like polyester" bow tie imitating the shape and coloring of such

standard butterflies as the Morning Cloak, the Eastern
Tailed Blue, and the Monarch, or, if you can't make up
your mind, the set of three can be had for $32? The or-
dinary telephone is always being improved, and many of
these improvements achieve instant success as BAD objects. One of the most recent is the Quacking Duck Phone
("as practical as it is beautiful"), which looks like a harmless
wooden decoy of a mallard duck. But when a call comes in,
it *quacks rather than rings,* and its *eyes light up* as well. It is
technologically as fancy as other BAD objects: "The
'quacker' is adjustable to high, low, and off."

Do you know those little soap receptacles that pro-
trude from the walls of showers? In no way bad. But in a
motel in West Hazleton, Pennsylvania, BAD has been
achieved: someone has had the bright idea of replacing
two of these innocuous soap dishes with plastic "clam-
shells" that stick out six inches, creating not just overcrowd-
ing in the shower stall but contusions and abrasions as well.
These obtrusive "shells" illustrate the close relation between BAD and cute, cuteness residing usually in the easy
act of making a thing much larger (the clamshell) or much
smaller (the twelve-inch *David*) than it should be.

Mickey Mouse began mouse size, but he has hypertrophied into human size and even larger, making him
cuter than ever. And speaking of Mickey, if you are a
"collector," you can acquire a "Limited Edition" four-inch-
high "Crystal Snow Globe" with a Mickey in the middle—
costumed as a sorcerer from his "role" in *Fantasia*—
surrounded by liquid in which, by shaking the globe, little
gold stars can be made to whirl about him. "A marvelous,
enchanting art object from a bygone era . . . an authentic
heirloom to save and treasure." The high value of this
object is attested by a "Serially Numbered Certificate of
Registration" included with each Snow Globe. Supremely
BAD pretenses like that indicate that we have arrived at

the ultimate suckerville, populated by ingenuous people who imagine themselves accumulating "collections" of valuable objects to pass on to their children. Thus it is necessary now to add an

Excursus on Collectibles

Contriving and mass-merchandising "collectibles" to be collected by "collectors" is an activity so contemporary that the term *collectibles* makes no appearance in dictionaries until the 1980s, when it is gingerly and politely defined, in *Webster's Ninth New Collegiate Dictionary* (1989), as signifying objects "that are collected by fanciers; especially . . . other than such traditionally collectible items as art, stamps, coins, and antiques." A more accurate definition, but a ruder one, would be "objects mass-marketed by the cynical for sale to dupes imagining that they are laying up 'exclusive' art objects which will increase in value and thus become valuable heirlooms to be passed on to grateful offspring."

It is the sellers' and advertisers' pretense that these collectible manufactures are valuable and/or artistic that qualifies them as BAD. The advertising for these ugly and worthless objects fills the pages of slick magazines aimed at the insecure middle class (see *BAD Advertising*), and the ads specialize in BAD language heavy with mock-archaic and pseudo-artistic terms like *heirloom* and *collection* ("Build your own heirloom collection"). Words appealing to snobbery and fake exclusivism abound: *First Edition, Limited Edition, exclusive, First Issue, work of art, masterpiece, authentic,* together with would-be dignifying snob adjectives appropriate (perhaps) to real art objects: *hand-crafted, richly detailed, legendary, magnificent,* and, most important, *valuable.* And the value is special, for, it is implied, it will surely increase in "years to come," when these objects will be treasured by "generations to come." And what are these precious items?

Porcelain thimbles, for a start. You can acquire valuable ones by joining the Thimble Collectors Club. (A standard way of merchandising BAD is to sell the customer the first item of "a series," which stimulates him to continue accumulating the rest as they come along.) Each month a member of the Thimble Collectors Club receives a china thimble said to be "an individual work of art," and the client is urged to "build a unique collection you'll treasure forever." After a while, you will be invited to invest in "a lovely glass-domed display stand" for your thimbles, "an attractive addition to the décor of your home."

This collection will be nice to pass on to your children—assumed, notice, to be fools as egregious as you are. You can pass on too a "Gold and Crystal Christmas Bell" with a Mickey Mouse clapper, "a true heirloom, sure to be enjoyed and treasured for generations," which has the additional merit of being a "First Edition." Or if you don't want to collect thimbles or crystal bells with golden Mickey Mouse clappers, how about a collection of fifteen small cat statuettes, in pewter, china, bronze, brass, and "crystal"? For these, you "subscribe," receiving a new cat statuette each month (only $30 each), and to show them off you get a "beautiful brass and glass *curio cabinet* for display."

That word *display* measures some of the pathos of the true collector of collectibles. Like the man who must invite an audience into his bathroom to watch him shave with his exquisite Waterford crystal–handled razor, the collector aims at approval and even respect by *displaying* the collection (every home a museum), and it's there that the collector's BAD comes in. (The seller's BAD lies in pretending that this tasteless junk is artistic and valuable.) A stand for display is an almost invariable attendant of these sad scams, making it clear that collectibles are acquired less to be valued for themselves or to bring their own delight to the possessor than to be seen and admired—an audience is always assumed, and soliciting the regard of that audience is the subtext of all these BAD transactions. The reasons why, and the reasons why "collecting" these contemptible objects is so much a stigma of the present moment, it would take a battalion of psychiatrists (allied with social workers) to explain.

If you're not grabbed by the Curio Cabinet Cats or perhaps regard them as not manly enough, you can collect swords, or at least "ten magnificent scale re-creations" of historic swords "from Caesar to the 20th Century," together with—of course—a "handsome hardwood wall display" case. These scaled-down artifacts come from "the definitive and official collection of the International Military Archives"—which is not well known outside of the ad campaign run by the "Franklin Mint," one of the shrewdest merchandisers of these BAD collectibles. As for other valuable objects in a series, you "subscribe" for these swords, and every three months one will arrive, whereupon you will disgorge $120. When the whole "set" is complete, you will be out $1,200, but you will have the satisfaction of conceiving of yourself as a collector of the finer things (macho department) and a thoughtful provider of a valuable legacy for your heirs. Macho desires are satisfied also by some table-sized BAD sculptures, made usually of "bonded" (i.e., bogus) bronze, and inevitably sentimental and artistically fourth-rate. Like the "Lone Sailor" statuette, "based on the original sculpture by Stanley Bleifield," an eight- or fifteen-inch-high representation of a U.S. sailor, hands in peacoat pocket, looking less courageous and resourceful than supremely bored and characterless. (The large original is BAD enough to be destined for the Navy Memorial in Washington. See *BAD Public Sculpture*.)

The fifteen-inch job will cost you $1,500, a small price to pay for a reputation as a collector of works of art.

There's also a seventeen-inch "masterpiece in bronze" by the well-known "Western" sculptor Buck McCain ("hailed by critics for his unerring accuracy"), depicting a mounted Crow Indian raising on high a buffalo skull in "solemn prayer" to "The Healing Spirit." And there's a "bonded bronze" statuette of Charles B. Macdonald, the famous golfer of the last century, modeled eight inches high by the great Alfred Petitto and shown wearing plus fours, jacket, and cap. Ugly beyond description. And if bronze doesn't fetch the collector of "sculpture," maybe "crystal" will:

> Now—for people who love fine crystal and the beauty of birds, Waterford is proud to introduce the Crystal Dove, the first issue of a new sculpture collection.

This three-inch-high glass bird, very clumsily modeled, will set the collector back $61.75—not really, when you think about it, a high price to pay for the eventual gratitude of the unborn: "For the collector, a valuable and distinctive addition to any treasured collection that will be cherished and appreciated for generations to come."

Ladies, to be sure, are more likely to fall for the crystal dovelet than gentlemen, but the male ego has not been neglected, and "crystal" can be offered in forms appealing to men both brand-name snobbish and art snobbish. For $1,195 you can "collect" a fifteen-inch-long solid glass model of the BMW 750iL, "evoking all those qualities connoisseurs of cars and crystal can imagine: power, prestige, and perfection." (A couple of hints for the psychiatrists there.) This glass auto is an "artistic" item offered only to "the most fastidious of collectors," and its authenticity is guaranteed by its having been "created under the careful supervision of BMW . . . designers."

Male collectors are assumed to be so devoid of decent skepticism and self-respect as to pay $33 for a nine-inch "collectible stein, handcrafted in fine ceramic," an "heirloom" issued in a "limited edition." It's really just a heavy, three-dimensional ad for Budweiser, with Anheuser-Busch logo and "The King of Beers" in colored raised relief. But even if it's only an ad, it assumes a profound understanding of the future: it knows that all the collector's heirs in "generations to come" will find that watery proletarian beer as tasty and wonderful as does the now-living collector himself.

Women collectors, on the other hand, are best seduced by expensive collectors' dolls, which tend to cost about $250 and which come with their own display stands, the whole package stimulating the copywriter to the most exquisite art. One doll calls forth this language:

> Her long silken hair, braided with faux pearls, cascades in folds of shimmering gold to her feet.

For confirmed TV viewers, there's a fourteen-inch Mr. Spock doll for only $75, "meticulously crafted in fine porcelain" and dressed in an "individually tailored uniform." This doll will arrive at your home "complete with its own stand, ready for home display." And this is just the first "issue" in the Star Trek Doll Collection: you will have the right to buy more dolls as they become available until your living room is filled with dolls on stands. The doll collectors would seem to overlap the collectors of "porcelain sculpture"—of ballet dancers, birds, and the more lovable animals—and the famous BAD hotel in Washington dealt with above (see *BAD Hotels*) proudly displays its collection of porcelain bird sculptures by the awful Helen Boehm, the "first lady of porcelain."

These examples of what the psychiatrists would call

the *libido ostentandi* ("will to display"), the urge to exhibit one's ownership of the meretricious, vividly illuminate the soul of the middle-class "collector." The wide gulf between what the collector hopes to convey to the audience ("mastery") and what actually is conveyed (suckerhood) is the gulf characteristic of all phenomena fit to be designated BAD.

There are collectors down below the middle class too, but they tend to go in for bad rather than BAD. An exemplary one is Texas auto dealer Jay Battenfield, who displays his collection of over 200,000 pearls; red, white, and blue beads; "every precious gemstone known to man"; bits of silver and gold; and "many collectors' items over 200 years old." Where does he display this collection? Pasted all over his car, a rebuilt 1963 Chevy Corvair Monza: this rich appliqué adds over a thousand pounds to the weight of the car and elicits admiration from a wide Texas audience. What distinguishes this busy collection and display from a BAD one is that Jay Buttenfield does not pretend to be a person of taste and probably has few plans to treasure up his Corvair for the benefit of his heirs.

"I think, therefore I am" used to do for seventeenth-century Europe. In late-twentieth-century America, it's rather "I consume, therefore I am." But we don't get to the heart of things unless we phrase it "I collect, therefore I am—and my children, who now treat me like dirt, will be grateful one day for the valuable heirlooms I'm currently laying up for them at great expense."

BAD PEOPLE

There are so many BAD people around that doing them justice would take a whole book, if not a library. Only a few examples can be considered here. Really BAD people tend to be in either politics or divinity. Both scenes require strenuous public manifestations of probity and virtue, and both thus involve a very wide gap between appearance and reality—the essential condition, as we have seen, for BAD. Jessie Helms comes to mind immediately, and so do Richard Nixon and his criminal attorney general John Mitchell; Edward Kennedy and Gary Hart, too. Among the reactionaries of Orange County, California, a popular toast is "To the Savior of Her Country, Mary Jo Kopechne," and another such toast could celebrate Gary Hart's girlfriend Donna Rice in the same terms. Numerous divines illustrate also the wide-gap BAD principle: Jimmy Swaggart, Jim Bakker, and the Reverend Sun Myung Moon, all of whom allowed the gap to grow too wide. But some people are BAD without being in any way either political or pious, like Bess Myerson, Zsa Zsa Gabor, and Leona Helmsley. Nor should we forget Ed Meese, James Watt, Morton Downey, Jr., Howard Cosell, and Oliver North and his faithful sidekick in obstructing justice, Fawn Hall. Then there are the horrible William Bennett, Judge Robert H. Bork, Geraldo Rivera, George Steinbrenner, and Sean Penn. Probably the current BAD champion is Kurt Waldheim: true, he's not an American, but he lived here long enough and received enough flattery to pass for a crypto-American. There's no doubt that BAD Don Ray Dixon is an American. He was the boss of the Vernon Savings and Loan, in Texas, and his houses and cowboy art collection and the whores he provided for the bank examiner cost us $1.3 billion. The only thing that saves Dan Quayle from a BAD label is that he's not showy enough yet—merely bad.

Should we run out of names, we can pick up more by noting the bumper stickers to be seen in the cultural backwaters of America, where we will find, among others,

> THANK GOD FOR AMERICANS LIKE JOHN WAYNE, PAUL HARVEY, & RONALD REAGAN.

The late baseball personality Billy Martin was certainly a bad type, and BAD too, despite his occasional entertainment value, as when he said things like "I'm getting sick and tired of people calling me a drunkard. I haven't had a drink in two days." Elvis Presley look-alikes and imitators like Bruce Borders, Steve West, Johnny Harra, and Toni

Roi are BAD people located at about the Billy Martin stratum.

All these can be named, but millions of BAD people are anonymous. These are the ones who chat during movies, plays, and concerts and write in library books.

BAD POETRY

If you have minimal literary talent but would like to acquire some of the prestige imputed, even today, to "poetry," a way to go is to produce works with socko-erotic beginnings, like

> A clitoris is a kind of brain
> —ALICE NOTLEY

> graciela wouldn't fuck me
> —TATIANA DE LA TIERRA

> I want you to be reading this, as I
> make love to your cock
> —LAURA CHESTER

> Whoever despises the clitoris despises
> the penis
> —MURIEL RUKEYSER

In Salisbury by the beach
my cock is swollen with love
of you
          —WALT CURTIS

I've been meeting men with big cocks lately
          —KEITH VACHA

and so on. And if you have no talent for coherence—
traditionally, the precise business of poetry, and even its
only business—you can assemble in any order all sorts of
items and present yourself as a "Surrealist":

buckets of blood in which the moon verbs are washed
giant boiled squid the remembrance of a lost
          constellation
                    —IVAN ARGÜELLES

The Surrealist act is easier if you make the lines shorter:

Thomas speech beyond
screed modern solace
          —TOM WEATHERLY

Or you can contrive a poem so impossible to read at the
outset that the uneducated will be struck with awe:

phantasmagorillaorgasmiasmacharismamama
diaphragmdiarrheacatarrhcatatoniccatastrophicmascara . . .
                    —CYN. ZARCO

Or you can use poetry to indulge in the party game of
Telling All and hoping the audience is interested:

i am a lesbian
          —JAN CLAUSEN

Or if your conception of the erotic is broad enough, you can startle the reader with an "Asshole Poem":

> It's about time someone ought to
> write a poem about assholes . . .
> —JIM HOLMES

Precious to BAD poets like these is membership in groups and schools: individually not very interesting, they lust for labels and designations and categories to impose upon themselves. Thus one such poet is said in a contributors note to have been born under the sign of "Sagittarius with a Capricorn cusp."

Another of these poet-joiners is said to be "a leading figure of the New York 'language' group." Others are proud to be tagged "passionate environmentalists," "Buddhist animal rights activists," or members of the "beyond Baroque group." An "urban Surrealist" is a designation treasured by one, a "New York realist" by another, and one woman is proud to have "strong affinities with the San Francisco erotic feminists." Some of these people's feeble sense of self-respect prompts them to conglobulate in quasi-Soviet *collectives* (cf. Vladimir Nabokov: "Intellectuals do not join groups"): thus one poet, according to a biographical note, "*belongs to* [my emphasis] the National Coalition of Black Lesbians and Gays . . . and New Words Bookstore Collective." Another "is a . . . member of the *Feminary* editorial collective." And (no surprise) there are New Age overlaps, with many of these BAD poets claiming interests in "occult art," shamanism and "Yogic philosophy," "magick," and "herbology." These pseudo-learned concerns do not, alas, prevent frequent sub-freshman grammatical blunders from marring otherwise plausible earnest performances, like Anne Waldman's errant participle,

drinking strong *genmai* tea
a purple hairpin slips to the floor,

and Sandi Castle's "presidential" innocence about the difference between *lie* and *lay,* as in

> When sleeping with them
> you know . . . men
> almost immediately following masturbation
> I lay in a prone position
> throw the covers off the bed
> and spend the night mothering them instead.

And then there's Christina M. Duncan's total deconstruc-
tion of syntax and sense:

> Now hurriedly we clamor while running to and fro
> As daily to our duties our energy to grow.

(Cf. Ezra Pound: "Poetry should be at least as well written
as prose.")
   Those things are BAD because they are Illiterate Pretentious. Other poems qualify because they represent the
Self-Satisfied or Cute:

> Oh God Forbid
> Oh God Forbid
> Oh God Forbid
>   Your Son
>   Your Son
>   Your Son
> Is Married
> Is Married
> Is Married
>   To A
>   To A

To A
Black Fairy
Black Fairy
Black Fairy

Oh God Forbid Your Son Is Married To A Black Fairy.
—FREDDIE GREENFIELD

Other BAD genres include the Politically or Socially Aggrieved ("This is the age of self-pity"—Anthony Powell) and the Desperately Egotistical, or Nobody Loves Me.

Faced with all these examples of BAD, the merely bad comes as a distinct relief, and one turns to the newly popular Cowboy Poetry with at least the satisfaction that one is not in the hands of a group (or "collective") of con men and women:

THE TWO THINGS IN LIFE THAT
I REALLY LOVE

by Gary McMahan

There's two things in life
That I really love:
That's women and horses,
This I'm sure of.
So when I die,
Please tan my hide
And tool me into
A saddle so fine.
And give me to a cowgirl
Who likes to ride,
So in the hereafter
I may rest
Between the two things
That I love best.

That's a real smiler and tear-jerker, with its sexiness implied instead of loudly asserted and its happy distance from political positions that everyone recognizes as gratifyingly correct. "The Two Things in Life That I Really Love" at least cannot be said, to quote from the back of Carol Rumen's *Making for the Open: The Chatto Book of Post-Feminist Poetry,* to "illuminate broad issues of human rights—between countries as well as individuals." Those who dimly remember the poems of Yeats and Eliot, not to mention George Herbert and Robert Herrick, will recall that poetry has nothing to do with "broad issues." Latching verbal art onto them guarantees that both the art and the issues will come out BAD.

BAD PUBLIC SCULPTURE

"Public" here means designed to be seen outdoors by large numbers of nonartistic people, from whom it would be unfair to expect taste or criticism. Here, BAD implies the usual third-rate and pretentious, and it also implies that the objects in question are respectfully received as great favors vouchsafed the populace by the community or the state. The prime example is the Statue of Liberty, that archetypal manifestation of the national yearning for kitsch. Its torch that *actually lights up* provides that novelty feature of pseudo-literalism that always excites lovers of BAD. The show-off size and irrelevance of J. G. Borglum's carvings on Mount Rushmore, the coarse neo-Egyptian hypertrophy of the whole operation, make that achievement an easy runner-up to the vulgarities of Miss Liberty (see *BAD Language*). Besides constituting a tribute to American gigantism—if you can't have quality, get quantity (see *BAD Hotels, BAD Engineering,* and *BAD Colleges and Universities*)—Borglum's Folly, in its unimaginative repre-

sentationalism, also celebrates philistine artistic retrogres-
sion and reaction (see *BAD Objects*). Seen from whatever
angle and from whatever distance, these four immense
heads deliver a message popular with the culturally aggrieved and uneducated: "Down with Modernism!" It's a
native version of Soviet Realism, aimed similarly at our
peasant class.

Although not really outdoors (it's just that the pompous immensity of the lobby it's in makes it seem like the
outdoors), the outsized "gold-toned" head of John F.
Kennedy in Washington's Kennedy Center (see *BAD Architecture*) is in the same tradition, the attempt to earn easy
awe from the multitude by sheer size (the World Trade
Center in New York comes to mind), and in this as in other
respects the immense BAD Kennedy head compares with
the ten-foot-tall head of Benjamin Franklin emplaced outside a firehouse in Philadelphia. The main interest here is
the thousands of pennies stuck onto this work, donated by
schoolchildren in their innocence.

But for sheer witlessness we turn from these Brob-
dingnagian artifacts to sculptures more "lifelike," that is,
human-sized. Here the name to conjure with is J. Seward
Johnson, who specializes in works whose appeal is the resemblance of the bronze figures—fully clothed in the styles
of twenty years ago—to those in wax museums. "Lifelikeness" is the aim, and these creepy metal mannequins sit on
benches reading bronze newspapers or raise bronze um-
brellas as they try to hail cabs just like the real people
Johnson hopes they will be confused with. Johnson has
explained his aim in making these vacuous simulacra: "I
would love people to say, 'How truly human . . . !' " The
problem is what Johnson means by *people*: real civilized
people, or six-year-old dull normals?

But it's a question whether vulgar representationalism
or facile "abstraction" produces the worst public sculpture.

Pretentious titles for abstractions are usually a tip-off that unignorable BAD is present, and such titles urge the sassy young to acts of rude travesty. On one university campus there is a fifty-foot-tall pair of leaning tubes, ten feet in diameter, painted various shades of red and orange, and apparently struggling with each other. The maker has named it *The Covenant*. Students wisely call it *Dueling Tampons*. In New York, sculptor Barnard Rosenthal's *Five in One* has earned from the locals the name *Giant Pile of Rusted Lids*, while Richard Serra's *Tilted Arc* is referred to as *That Ugly Fucking Wall*. A moral question bound to surface among the more intelligent viewers of these BAD sculptures is whether in their case vandalism isn't justified, isn't, indeed, a public duty. There are said to be groups of people of taste and sense designating themselves Art Commandos, whose mission is the defacement and, if possible, the destruction of these eyesores. One person thinking of membership in this group has decided, after long thought, that he won't join—not for moral but for artistic reasons. "Vandalism," he says, "is no solution: bad sculpture actually looks worse when defaced."

Of one city, a local observer writes:

> Though guidebooks love to point out that Philadelphia has more public art than any other city in the country, they rarely mention something far more significant: a high percentage of our public art is not merely bad but absolutely embarrassingly bad.

(That writer, and more power to him, seems to be groping toward the idea of BAD.) One item on proud display in that city has been called by an eminent critic "the single worst sculpture of the twentieth century," a distinction hard to beat. One creator of this BAD public trash has confessed. Sculpture, he now says, "was one of my worst subjects at school. I didn't have any feeling for it at all."

The whole movement by universities, corporations, and municipalities to install public sculpture seems an attempt to out-Medici the Medicis. But one thing is fatally missing. Taste. Just as one thing is fatally missing in the sculptors. Talent. And one thing is missing in the audience. Courage to ridicule and object.

BAD RESTAURANTS

Restaurants can be classified, reading up from low to high, as bad, good, and BAD, and once you reach the top, *restaurant* and *fakery* are virtually synonymous. "An evening on the town, which used to mean dinner and a show, now means," says Barbara Ehrenreich, "a showy dinner."

If you are alert and have not had too many drinks beforehand, you can generally pick up signals of a BAD place before entering. The word *gourmet* appearing anywhere is a trustworthy warning, and you're not entirely safe with *bistro* either. Another signal is the kind of cars parked in front or in an adjoining lot. As critic Holly Moore has perceived, the presence of lots of "good" (i.e., expensive) cars is a sign of BAD, while a plethora of ten-year-old Chevies and Saabs and even a handful of pickup trucks conveys the message that the food may be just OK. If there are no cars nearby and if some coarse adolescents can be seen hanging around the front of the establishment, unshaven and groping their crotches, it can be inferred that the restaurant goes in for that invariable sign of BAD, "valet" parking. This is to gratify people so pompous and self-regarding that they feel their dignity impugned if they have to park their own car and walk back two blocks. Actually, valet parking is less "for your convenience," as its entrepreneurs like to put it, than for the restaurant's convenience—and your exploitation. The object is to make you feel important (especially in front of your dinner guests) and to tempt you, once inside, to order lavishly and tip like a big spender—which will tempt you to tip in the same style when you finally retrieve your car (after a long wait) from the dirty boys.

So BAD have things become that valet parking is a significant sign of the times. It appeals to ostentatious and at the same time insecure people who like to imagine that they give off an aristocratic aura and who conceive that unless they receive "service" at all times, they risk losing caste. They don't perceive that today most "service" (hotel room-service is a prime example) is an inconvenience and a bore, a distinct inhibition on one's freedom and dignity. Lewis H. Lapham has come upon a valet-parking brochure issued by a company in Los Angeles which implies the whole socially embarrassing story. Valet parking, we read, is now "the ultimate parking service," not just at restaurants but for parties at home as well. "Valet parking is no longer a luxury for home entertaining. It has become an expected and welcome service, as it sets the tone of the party and sends the guests away at the end of the evening feeling very special and nurtured." There, acute readers will infer the very BAD American tendency to buy esteem instead of earning it.

Instructed by the above, you have now parked your car yourself and, having noted with misgivings that no menu is posted outside (another sign of BAD), you have decided to chance it this time and actually enter. More

BAD signals may now confront you, like signs reading "Proper Attire Requested" (see *BAD Signs*) and a head-waiter (in BAD restaurants, always referred to as the Metra Dee) wonderfully combining greasy obsequiousness with contempt. He will show you to a table, seat you, and if the restaurant is particularly BAD, remove your napkin (one-half polyester) from its place on the table, shake it out showily, and deploy it on your lap, it being assumed that this "service" is what you treasure.

The next warning of BAD will be the menu. If it is very large and heavy and bound in padded mock leather with tassels, look out: someone is about to be shafted. Good sense would suggest that the wine list already be on the table, like the cutlery and glasses. In BAD restaurants it is not but is finally and ostentatiously brought by a sommelier, an unnecessary and BAD employee. If the wine list is "presented" at this time, you will notice that BAD restaurants like to omit vintage years and shippers' names, assuming that no customer knows or cares about these things and that in an atmosphere of vagueness and pretense ("Proper Attire Requested"), overpricing will pass without notice—especially since the restaurant knows that anyone entering it after all the warning signs is a snob and an ass, too ignorant and insecure to complain about anything. And for the still hopeful, by the time the red wine arrives in its basket it will be too late to leave without being arrested.

A general principle about BAD menus is that the more extensive, the worse. These pander to the sacred American conviction that vast "choice" among the third-rate is superior to limited choice among the good. But in addition to the irrelevant multitudinousness, it will be the language of the menu that will be the main augury of BAD to come. Here as everywhere, metaphors and purple adjectives will be the tools of hype and fraud, and novel diction will seek to suggest up-to-dateness, presumed to be a good thing. Thus one will read that certain dishes, as if they were part of a "fashion" "collection," have been *designed by* or *created by* someone who works in the kitchen, and at the end of the virtually endless menu, you will read that "Our desserts will be *showcased* to you by your server." If a dessert is listed on the menu, it will not just be listed: it will be celebrated in terms dear to practitioners of *BAD Advertising* (q.v.):

> A Dark Treasure Chest filled with White Nugget Chocolate Mousse and Jewels of Fresh Fruit on a Golden Pond of Crème Anglais with tiny Comets of Chopped Hazelnuts and Red Raspberries.

(And you can be sure that in a BAD restaurant no diner will have the guts to risk shame by inquiring what *Crème Anglais* is, or risk a beating-up by observing to the Metra Dee that regardless of what it is, *Anglais* is illiterate BAD for *Anglaise*.)

As that example helps indicate, the menu will assume an entirely ignorant clientele, for BAD cannot flourish in the face of either knowledge or courage. The best-known classic dishes will be elaborately defined for the BAD diners (it takes two to play), and various come-on modifiers and substantives appropriate to BAD lyric poems—or advertising—will be brought into play. I quote some from one menu: *elegant, delicate, creamy, aroma, art, fragrance*; and "Three poached pink prawns joyfully dance their way through a light sauce of sweet lemon juice." BAD language like that skillfully disguises from the unimaginative, the ignorant, and the credulous the actual mass production and off-premises preparation presided over by chefs more notable for cunning than for talent or honor. Increasingly popular among such are totally prepared frozen entrees bought in quantity from a central restaurant-supply house

and quickly microwaved in the kitchen by someone sporting a showy *toque blanche* (see *BAD Objects*) but possessing
rather the attributes of an engineer than a cook. The pretense remains that these dishes have been lovingly prepared right there in your honest and friendly kitchen
behind the screen. The menus of BAD restaurants are
largely determined not by what tastes good but by what
freezes well—like lobster tails and carrot cake. And that is
true even in politically and socially self-righteous restaurants, "ethnic" and other, which will provide on request
their menu in Braille.

And in the same way a skilled sleight-of-hand artist
can "force" a card on the unsuspecting, a skilled menu
writer can force on the innocent a given dish (usually a
highly profitable one calling for cheap ingredients and
little preparation) by invoking the graphic arts—design,
placement, and typography: a box of heavy rule around
the restaurant's most loathsome dish has been found to
work wonders. Many restaurateurs secretly agree that their
hapless customer can be led to choose the items placed
either first or last in the list of entrees, and that's where
they position the ones they want to move. And in considering labor costs, experienced managers of restaurants
have found that unless you charge a lot, careful presentations on the plate are uneconomical. One manager recently explained why he dropped rack of lamb from the
menu. It was still popular, but he found it took "well over
a minute" for "someone to plate." (*Plate* as a verb is part of
the jargon of kitchens, seldom revealed to customers—
except when a new waiter forgets and employs behind-the-
scenes idiom to impatient diners asking where their meal
is: "Your dinners will arrive right away: your *on-trays* are
being plated now."

The sad thing is that so many indexes of BAD are
available only after you've sat down and committed your-

self to staying. Like tableside cooking, involving great fire effects from flambés, Baked Alaskas, and the like. Recently the following unironic words appeared in the restaurant section of a BAD newspaper:

> There was a time when cooking at tableside was the personal art of hotel and restaurant captains, maitre d's and even waiters. Today, it is becoming increasingly difficult to find restaurants featuring this indulgence.

That belongs not in the restaurant section but in the Thank God! Department. Just as a sports team dresses in the dressing room before playing on the field, just as actresses make up behind the set, cooking belongs in the kitchen. Better junk or take-out food than the ostentatious BAD flames all over the dining room. The always acute Ada Louise Huxtable observes, "In America the pendulum swings from cheap expediency to cheap pretense; there is nothing, for example, between fast food and foolish flambé."

There's another indicator of BAD regrettably unavailable until you've committed yourself. That is Pretty Presentation, by the imperatives of which each plate must ape a painting—usually a BAD abstraction but sometimes a sentimental land- or seascape. In really top-BAD premises, visual presentation takes over entirely, and you get the impression that the eye, not the mouth, is the organ being addressed. Like Huxtable, Tom Wolfe has a sharp eye for BAD, and it is to him that we owe one of the most successful rebukes of BAD plate décor. In *The Bonfire of the Vanities,* the British writer Peter Fallow is the guest of Arthur Ruskin at the highly popular BAD restaurant La Boue de Argent:

> The first course arrived. Fallow had ordered a vegetable pâté. The pâté was a small pinkish semicircle with

stalks of rhubarb arranged around it like rays. It was
perched in the upper left-hand quadrant of a large
plate. The plate seemed to be glazed with an odd Art
Nouveau painting of a Spanish galleon on a reddish
sea sailing toward the . . . sunset . . . but the setting sun
was, in fact, the pâté, with its rhubarb rays, and the
Spanish ship was not done in glaze at all but in different colors of sauce. It was a painting in sauce.

And the trade actually calls it "sauce painting," and certain
chefs, greatly in demand, specialize in it. Arthur Ruskin's
plate is equally impressive: his (which "he took no notice
of")

contained a bed of flat green noodles carefully inter-
twined to create a basket weave, superimposed upon
which was a flock of butterflies fashioned from pairs of
mushroom slices, for the wings; pimientos, onion
slices, shallots, and capers, for the bodies, eyes, and
antennae.

Similar to this BAD practice but motivated less by paint-
erly affectations than a misplaced lust for novelty, no matter how awful the results, is never serving roast beef, say,
or lamb chops without ranging a number of white grapes
alongside, or never serving grilled salmon without seeing
to it that a few slices of canned grapefruit keep it company.
It is in restaurants like these that you can count on being
touted by mobile sellers of roses for the lady; prints, en-
gravings, charcoal sketches, and watercolors; and jewelry.
And in most BAD restaurants there will be strolling mu-
sicians (bad rather than BAD), whose office is to receive
money for preventing conversation.

The right sort of waiters and waitresses make an important contribution to BAD, largely by telling you their
first names ("Hi! My name is Brad. I'm your server for

tonight, and—"), followed by the protracted recitation of "our specials this evening," preferably with no prices indicated. The point of reciting instead of printing a large part of the menu is twofold: to entice the client into high, if vague, expenditure, few diners being so rude or so brave as to require the waiter to go back and announce, now, the price for each item; and to establish at the very outset a quasi-"friendly" relation between waiter and customers, which, if successful, will mean that the diners will probably not be distressed when the service is BAD and will be ready to forgive gaffes or oversights when committed by someone who is practically a member of the family.

Waiters and waitresses are taught to be more than order-takers and plate-bearers. They are taught to become, like most Americans, salespersons of BAD. Judi Radice, director of marketing for a group of restaurants based in San Francisco, has declared, "We want waiters to merchandise the menu." Thus, rather than saying "Will you have dessert?" a waiter will say "May I bring you a delightful, rich serving of our superb chocolate mousse?" The ostentatious deployment during the meal of an outsized pepper mill is also a bid for an illusion of waiter-diner intimacy. Marian Burros, restaurant critic of the *New York Times*, says, "The invasion of the giant pepper mills has gotten out of hand." Why not have a giant (to prevent stealing) pepper grinder on each table so that, as Burros says, "I could decide for myself, *after* I have taken a bite"? But if that happened, you'd not owe a significant debt of thanks to the waiter, as you incur also when, laying down each plate, he exhorts you to "Enjoy!"

Most BAD waiters and waitresses, obliged to pretend that mock friendliness will substitute for professional dignity, can be said to occupy that "psychologist's wonderland," as Cyril Connolly has called it, "which is revealed to us when we watch charmless people trying to be charming." The remedy, if difficult, is clear: don't try to be charming. But to follow that injunction would put an end to all sorts of BAD.

Students of restaurant BAD master early in their experience one important principle, which can be called Brian Miller's Law, after the New York food critic who has called attention to it: the higher the physical elevation of the restaurant, the more likely that it will be BAD. Good examples are the restaurants high atop world's fair erections, whose main interest is not in food but in revolving. Once the high-elevation principle is understood, airline food and service no longer present a puzzle. The problem here is the problem in all "stunt" victualing, where food is served triumphantly in impossible situations—like in treehouses, tiny boats, and under severe artillery fire. In cases like these, we are supposed to marvel not at the food but at the degree to which difficulties have been overcome. Airline feeding presents a pure example of BAD. Why try to serve *saumon en croûte* when you could do tuna salad perfectly well? Best of all would be honest sandwiches, followed by ice-cream bars—and BAD would receive a humiliating setback.

BAD SIGNS

Not portents, symbols, emblems, or arcane semiotic signifiers but posted public messages for all to read and react to. The simply bad signs are the sweet, barely literate ones, those that play fast and loose with the apostrophe ("Watermelon's"), go in for folk spelling *(potatoe),* or use quotation marks to indicate emphasis:

> POSITIVELY
> "NO TRESPASSING"

That sort of thing is perfectly harmless, and in the long run does no discredit to human nature.

Very different are BAD signs. They are openly offensive, characterized by pseudo-precision, euphemism or outright fraud—and cuteness. Perhaps the best-known is the multilane highway sign DO NOT CROSS MEDIAN DIVIDER and its many verbose variants. Nine syllables there (see

BAD Language), certainly an improvement in weight, length, and pomposity (presumably a consideration when drivers are reading signs at eighty miles per hour) over the mere four syllables of, say, KEEP OFF GRASS STRIP, or the three of KEEP OFF GRASS, or even the childishly simple DO NOT CROSS.

But at least that sort of BAD sign causes little confusion. A usage combining the pretentious with the cute is contriving unique designations for commercial addresses and then acting as if the mystery location of the premises were obvious. Vanity addresses, these are called. Like a big sign reading Six (never simply 6) Arroyo Place (actually 1435 Orange Grove Avenue), or one saying Five Penn Plaza (actually 1617 Walnut Street). The telephone book often retains some honesty, providing the actual address, but sometimes it enjoys frustrating the searcher, requiring a phone call to the business in question: "Where *are* you?" And the clever vanity-address deviser can come up with even more vague designations. As Route 1 passes through northern New Jersey, the traveler will come upon a roadside structure labeling itself—very snazzy, this—One Dental Plaza. How is he to infer that it is actually 475 Rte. 1, Franklin Park, NJ?

Another kind of BAD pseudo-precision is increasingly met with, and its effect is to make life a little harder for everyone. This involves the free deployment of unexplained abbreviations and acronyms. Communication is nicely impeded by signs or public announcements like this one, devised by the American Red Cross:

[Baby holding up sign:]

> IMPORTANT:
>
> Please hug me, feed me,
> keep me warm, and PLEASE
> learn American Red Cross
> Infant and Child CPR.

CPR is not elucidated. How can we learn it if it won't tell us what it is? For some reason, the health (these days, "wellness") trade especially goes in for these three-letter showoff puzzles. HMO, for example: I had to ask twenty people what it meant until some kind soul in the know told me. One ad in an urban bus reads:

> HAVING A BABY?
>
> MSP has free health care
> for pregnant women.

MSP is carefully unexplained. These initials and acronyms are presumably there to make those who present them seem desirably up-to-date, even "scientific," and sometimes attractively "military." Their real function is to be BAD rather than to communicate. In the same way, one sees implicitly self-congratulatory signs promising nice things to *Senior Citizens* without any indication of what those words mean: over fifty-five? sixty? sixty-three? sixty-five? seventy or over? The hapless senior must ask each time what the sign means, and if the bus or subway sign reads

SENIOR CITIZENS RIDE FREE OFF-PEAK HOURS

the poor old person will be further puzzled, no one informing him what peak hours are. The restaurant and bar sign PROPER ATTIRE REQUESTED is of course a similar cause of puzzlement. To infer what it means, you'd have to know a lot about the social class and background of the spokesman. Does he or she mean T-shirts and khakis, jacket and tie, business suits, or what? May Levi's be worn if clean and pressed? Or is the sign simply saying, "This notice gives us the right to throw you out if we don't happen to like you"? Impossible to tell exactly what's meant, but the causes of both bullying and vagueness have been well served.

If you manage to pass that sign satisfactorily and penetrate to the interior of the restaurant or bar, you will be in a position to gauge the degree of Toilet Shame operating there. Toilet Shame occasions the assiduous hiding of the toilets, which requires contriving for them the tiniest, least conspicuous, or most misleading signs. If you took the shameless, adult principle of the French *pissoirs* and turned it entirely inside out, you'd have something like the attitude governing the shamefaced hiding of the toilets in public America. Often, of course, the motive is more than shame: it's to prevent the indigent, the mad, the homeless, or the nonpaying from obtaining any relief. (Where, by the way, do the homeless in cities *go* to do number two?) But if Toilet Shame is rife in America, we are still well behind China in the intensity of our shame. The Chinese apparently regard body functions as so unspeakably shameful that the toilets have no signs at all and furthermore are hidden away in the most derelict and shame-making back areas, unlikely ever to be discovered but by those in the shameful know.

You might think that construction workers, the very incarnation of macho-hood, notorious for voicing rude and lustful sentiments at passing women and generally achieving a reputation for calling a spade a spade, would frequent a world where a toilet is called a *toilet*. But what do we find? Toilet shame even on the construction site, with the movable one-holers designated never *toilet,* but, cutely,

> Porto-Potty
> Potty Queen
> Por-to-let
> Sani-John
> B. F. I. [cute for Biffy]

and the like. What a jolt to masculinity to enter one of those, whose designations are as cute as those indicating men's and women's toilets in (usually BAD) restaurants and bars. Some of these signs require considerable interpretation before you feel secure in opening one door and not the other. How about "Pointers" and "Setters" for self-conscious cuteness?

In cuteness (see *BAD Language*), that's comparable to the usage in some of the commuters' railway parking lots in the Washington suburbs, which designate the lane where only a brief stop to discharge passengers is permitted—what would you guess? the No-Parking Lane? the Brief Stopping Only Lane? No. The sign calls it the "Kiss and Ride" lane. And for real show-off cuteness which a previous age would have regarded as blasphemous instead of merely stupid, how about the sign near the Houston airport at Christmastime, "Happy Birthday, Jesus!"?

Like *toilet,* other words are considered too shameful for signs, and one risks nemesis by uttering them. My nearby bank was robbed one morning and the doors were shut for the rest of the day. A sign, ready-printed for this sort of emergency, was posted at the front door:

THIS BANK IS CLOSED UNTIL
FURTHER NOTICE FOR THE
FOLLOWING REASON: _____ .

But the blank was carefully not filled in, the word *Robbery* being too awful to be conveyed. That sign suggests something worth pondering. This is not, as is often asserted, the age of the Information Explosion. It's the age of the Publicity, or Disinformation, Explosion. Or if we are presented with information, it tends to be of the sort conveyed by bumper stickers like "I [heart] My Dog," pretending to deliver an interesting message but actually testifying only to the affixer's pathetic need to amount to something in a society so stupid that a self-proclaimed love of animals is held to be near the top of moral and social virtues.

If shame attends thoughts of toilets and robberies, none whatever seems to attach to gestures of sexual self-advertisement. In recent years, legible clothing (Alison Lurie's nice phrase), especially the T-shirt with language on it, has evolved dramatically from a mere readable garment associating the wearer with the success of Coke or Coors or Gatorade to an attention-getting (no, attention-demanding) public sign advertising one's readiness to plunge into sex at any time or place. (Example: LET'S FUCK.) The word *suck* and its cognates seem indispensable to the current T-shirt-as-sign, and one T-shirt issued by Verne's Clambake House, Terre Haute, Indiana, invites its readers to

LICK ME, SUCK ME, EAT ME ALL NIGHT LONG.

Unthinkable except in the age of BAD, that is, the age of rampant publicity, would be a T-shirt affected by preg-

nant women reading, at breast level, BABY, with an arrow
pointing downward to the protruding belly. A similar lust
to make public what was formerly private is the T-shirt
reading I'M WITH STUPID, with an arrow indicating the
wearer's hapless spouse (here, you have to be careful to get
him or her to walk on the appropriate side). A T-shirt sign
designed to earn you a reputation as a bold wag is one
reading GONE FISHING. Innocent enough, one might think,
but this one depicts a man with a happy smile holding a
fishing rod at the edge of a pond. Below his waist, his
catch, a large fish and the occasion of his joy, is shown
engaged in a rare act of fellatio. And when do tattoos enter
the category of public signs? The small anchor or "Mother"
or the mere "Death Before Dishonor" can be forgiven. But
when the tattoo tries to become the center of attention, it
verges on the bad; and when it takes over the whole area—
coiled boa constrictor on the chest, etc.—and implies a
statement like "I am interesting. Look at me," then it becomes BAD.

Travelers of all kinds are the usual addressees and
victims of BAD signs, like the immense illuminated sign
visible from trains crossing the Delaware at Trenton, New
Jersey. Here the urge to be cute and to contrive a rhyme
results in idiomatic disaster:

> TRENTON MAKES THE WORLD TAKES

Takes? Is *buys* meant? *Uses*? *Enjoys*? But not *takes*, surely.
Cuteness has caused that.

But other causes of BAD signs are sheer dumbness
and want of imagination. Consider the rhetorical ineptitude of some of the information boards in Amtrak stations, which quietly reverse the normal usage of indicating

the direction of trains FROM somewhere TO somewhere and list the destination first, causing untold confusion and error. And it would be hard to find a more telling example of American doltishness and provincialism than a sign in a large East Coast airport greeting arriving foreign travelers and instructing them in Spanish, German, French, and English how to manage the luggage carts provided. It's important to understand that this is in the immigration-control area, well before people arrive at the bank window. To get a cart, you have to insert a dollar in the device locking them. And the sign? It says, "Do Not Use Foreign Currency." This, says journalist Clark DeLeon, is a fine example of "bush-league" behavior in a city with "world-class pretensions"—a memorable example of pure BAD in action. (And see *BAD Airports.*)

Probably because of the severe deterioration of intellectual training here (see *BAD Colleges and Universities*), an increasingly common sign betrays innocence of the elementary rhetorical principle that phrases tend to convey less detachable meaning than clauses, and dependent elements less than independent. Sometimes experienced writers are seduced into delivering embarrassingly incomplete clauses as if they were saying something. Mortimer J. Adler titled one of his books *We Hold These Truths*: in the absence of the words *to be self-evident*, etc., the reader unfamiliar with the rest of the sentence is left asking, "OK, you consider these truths to be *what*? Be specific!" But perhaps, and this is not easy to believe, Dr. Adler has forgotten that *hold* here does not mean *grasp* or *treasure* but something close to *regard*. Whatever the reason, the result is BAD—showy and empty.

This habit of portentous incompletion might be termed, by those learned in current literary theory, *non-closure*. In the poems of John Ashbery—which seldom seem "completed" in the old sense—the technique is celebrated as *indeterminacy*. It is celebrated, that is, by theorists. Readers might consider it, on the other hand, evidence of preciousness or even ineptitude. "Stretching beyond one's literary means and falling, therefore, on one's ass" might be a nonliterary-theoretical way of putting it, and the appropriateness of that coarse designation may be seen in the following examples of BAD signs. They illustrate the liability of enthusiasts both religious and patriotic to extend themselves beyond their capacity and to be punished by comic rhetorical pratfalls. In printed matter this would be pathetic, but when blown up into immense signs visible for blocks, and often lighted up at night, the inept vainglory is hilarious.

Here's a lulu, surely a classic of indeterminacy. This is a sign on a building housing the Newman Center at a university:

IN THE BEGINNING GOD

God *what*? What did he *do*? Come clean! That has a corollary in the sweatshirts and baseball caps worn by religious fundamentalists:

NO GREATER LOVE

Than what? What *are* you talking about? And the patriotic temptation to portentousness can hustle the pretentious into nonsense just as surely as the religious. Celebrating the bicentenary of the Constitution, the official sloganeers came up with this little bit of open-endedness, which found its way onto thousands of T-shirts, posters, bumper stickers, lapel buttons, and prole caps:

WE THE PEOPLE

Something missing there, isn't there? Perhaps the verb?
We the People what?

All these offer ample evidence of BAD: pretense, va-
cuity, the flight from meaning, together with the exhi-
bitionism that prompts BAD writers to blazon their
ignorance before the largest audience. It's worth noticing
that the wearers of lewd T-shirts, who seem to know exactly what message they want to convey and to be interested in conveying it, always complete the message.
Whatever they may be, they are at least masters (and mis-
tresses) of "closure."

BAD TELEVISION

Although now and then it tries to cover its shame and put on airs, television is a grossly proletarian medium, efficient at merchandising denture cleansers and incontinence diapers, beer, laxatives, cars, and laundry supplies, but death to books, ideas, the sense of history, and the complexities, subtleties, and ironies of civilized discourse. Rehearsing for one talk show about "culture," I was asked to find an easy synonym for *anthropological,* a term, I was assured, way over the heads of the audience. This is why it's not the programs aiming at popular conceptions of "entertainment" that are BAD. Women's wrestling, *The Oprah Winfrey Show,* the childish prime-time sitcoms, the inflated dramatic "specials" where all characters act on comic-strip motivations—these are successfully bad, but hardly a threat to intelligence, since only the already lost could be found still watching after a thirty-second trial. It is certainly bad that more American households have TV sets than have flush toilets and that the average family watches seven and a half hours a day, which can mean every night from, say, 4:30 until midnight, absorbing the values of *Lifestyles of the Rich and Famous* and the artistic subtleties of *Alien Nation*. That's bad, but still not BAD.

For BAD, you'd turn first to the news shows where events are either sentimentalized or melodramatized to keep the watcher from switching channels until the heart of the matter, the next commercial, is arrived at. Equally BAD are the relentlessly middlebrow quasi-intellectual and pseudo-analytical news specials, where a "panel" disagrees with itself. Here, the illusion presides that the proceedings are as free as in any old locker or seminar room, but actually an inflexible set of personality clichés and *ad hominem* ideological conventions determines that nothing new or unsuperficial can take place. Lewis Lapham notes, "Despite its seeming fluidity, TV is a remarkably rigid medium that makes use of personae as immutable as the characters in the commedia dell'arte," another way of illuminating the distance between appearance and actuality always present in a case of BAD.

You can say of television today what Charles Lamb said of newspapers long ago: you never open one (i.e., turn on the set) without a slight thrill of expectation, and you never close one (i.e., turn the damned thing off) without disappointment. If you are at all bright, your initial slight titillation is rapidly overcome by the bromides and formulas, the constant victory of presentation over substance, the unremitting wheeling-out of the tried and tested instead of anything original. TV is a place where nothing exciting or interesting can possibly happen—except when sports are being broadcast live. *Will* the Indy car crash? *Will* a fight more interesting than usual break out on the basketball court? *Will* the Olympic ice-dancing couple slip and fall? *Will* that poleaxed football player get up, or will he be removed, apparently dead, from the field?

Moments like those might engage curiosity and, for a moment, satisfy, except that a voice is always butting in to comment, explain, relate, and certify—the play-by-play commentator must certify each play before we are presumed to understand what's going on. "It's a high fly to left field and Ryan is chasing it—back to the wall, back, back," etc., when we can see it perfectly well. The assumption is clear: nothing is real unless validated by commentary and interpretation.

The same ailment afflicts TV news. Everything must be made into a "story," even things clearly self-sufficient without commentary: a volcano going off, a whale surfacing, soccer fans beating each other up, fifteen wrecked cars strewn over a California thruway. Former newspaper reporter Tom Wolfe recognizes that TV does "set events" like these well, and he goes on to say that these and their like are all the "news" it should present. In fact, he says, "It'd be a service to the country if television news operations were shut down *totally* and they only broadcast hearings, press conferences, and hockey games. *That* would be television news. At least the public would not have the false impression that it's getting news coverage." As it stands now, TV news programs are the very essence of BAD: the gulf between the pretended and the actual is dramatized five times a week in the familiar self-introduction "Dan Rather *reporting,*" when usually he's not reporting at all but acting and reading—and reading from the TelePrompTer, as Lapham says, language "configured to the understanding of a six-year-old child." Rather's is a small deception, to be sure, a part of the tired world of show business masquerading as life that has been the material of TV from the outset. But even Dan Rather is contributing, as Todd Gitlin says, to "a way of life that has elevated banality and deception to cultural principles," for after all, if your main business is to sell largely worthless and un-

necessary products, mendacity and mediocrity must gov-
ern. They are not just unfortunate by-products of
television: they are its very reason for being.

So powerful is the pull of mendacity once profit enters
as a motive that it's now leaking into once-pure public
television from the openly mercantile and cynical channels. When public television has to admit that a powerful
commercial sponsor is behind a given program, which
means that certain interesting things can't be noticed or
said at all, its sense of shame impels it to avoid a phrase like
sponsored by in favor of euphemistic formulas like "This
program is made possible by *a grant* from," implying with
grant that the whole operation is taking place in the high-
minded, disinterested realm of foundations, universities,
and similar nontainted institutions.

Local TV news, as distinguished from national, tends
to be more bad than BAD. Where national news specializes
in single stars, like Rather or Peter Jennings, local news
requires its players to emphasize that none is preeminent;
instead, they are members of a "news team," which invari-
ably includes:

>   one woman (often Asian)
>   one black
>   one white male news reader
>   one white (sometimes black) sports news reader
>   one weather person, often a woman

The implication is that this group consists of just folks,
people no better, and surely no smarter, than you, but for
the moment trustworthy servants of authenticity. And
charm: local news programs like all else must survive on
the advertising that comes in, which means that they are
obliged to transform news into what used to be called
human-interest features—dogs and cats saved from burn-

ing buildings, siblings reunited after many years, golden weddings, funny coincidences. Todd Gitlin again: "The attitudes, feelings, values of 'the common people' are the bedrock standard to which all value is finally referred," and acting on those principles of successful mass merchandising, television has consummated a perfect fusion between the most cynical capitalism and the most sentimental populism. This fact, so little welcome to the sweet, goodhearted people who persist in believing television capable of a "cultural" contribution, is a reason why some get angry when TV is stigmatized as a prole medium. It *must* flatter the dumb and the credulous to do its job.

Despite the horrors that real life now and then obliges it to notice, television news is (like its print counterpart, *USA Today*) unfailingly optimistic, and its anchormen and -women are never far from the convention of obligatory show-biz smiles. The optimism of the commercials is indistinguishable from the optimism of the "reporting," and as Mark Crispin Miller has perceived, "in order for TV's ads to seem 'a bonus—not an intrusion,' the rest of television first had to change in many subtle ways, imperceptibly taking on the quality of the commercials." When "Tedd" Abramson named his champion white limo *The American Dream*, he was unwittingly illustrating Miller's point—that America's main contribution to the world is BAD. It is the thing that we are best at.

THE DUMBING

OF AMERICA

Thus, BAD. The United States especially overflows with it because of all countries it is the most addicted to self-praise and complacency—even more than France. "God intended for us to have the highest moral country in the world," declares Lisa Nelson, a nurse in Oregon quoted recently in *USA Today*. That widespread conviction has justified the American habit of not relinquishing its moral policemanship of such former colonies as Panama and the Philippines, whose accused are hauled back to the untainted jurisdiction of "the Mainland" for trial and hoped-for disgrace. The USA is the world headquarters of moral pretension. The American habit of regarding itself for almost half a century as the Leader of the Free World (and thus superb and a model in all respects for the less fortunate) has made it easy for Americans to ignore certain unpleasant facts. Like the current rate of adult illiteracy— an admitted 40 percent in the large city I live in, and doubtless higher. Indeed, of the 158 countries comprising the United Nations, the United States ranks only forty-

ninth in literacy. The Census of 1990 ran into trouble for
a surprising reason: a very great many people, coming
upon the census form dropped through their mail slot,
threw it out simply because they couldn't read it, just as
they can't read any English prose, including the story of
the Three Bears or Cinderella. These are the people in a
train station who have to ask bystanders what track the
train for Rochester is on because they can't read the notice
board. And there are lots of people who can't read a clock
face: these stop you on the street to ask you the time. It's
not that they can't afford a watch: they can't interpret what
it says.

Yes, yes, you say—these are "minorities" or other
members of the visible underclass, and it's all too bad. But
the group of *60 million* functionally illiterate includes many
like the professional described by Jonathan Kozol in *Illiterate America*. Meticulous and eminently presentable, this
man works in New York:

> He gets up in the morning, showers, shaves, and
> dresses in a dark gray business suit, then goes downstairs and buys a New York *Times* from the small newsstand on the corner of his street. Folding it neatly, he
> goes into the subway and arrives at work at 9 A.M.
>
> He places the folded New York *Times* next to the
> briefcase on his desk and sets to work on graphic illustrations for the advertising copy that is handed to
> him by the editor who is his boss.
>
> "Run over this with me. Just make sure I get the
> gist of what you really want."
>
> The editor, unsuspecting, takes this as a reasonable request. In the process of expanding on his copy,
> he recites the language of the text: a language that is
> instantly imprinted on the illustrator's mind.
>
> At lunch he grabs the folded copy of the New
> York *Times,* carries it with him to a coffee shop, places
> it beside his plate, eats a sandwich, drinks a beer, and
> soon heads back to work.

> At 5 P.M. he takes his briefcase and his New York
> *Times,* waits for the elevator, walks two blocks to catch
> an uptown bus, stops at a corner store to buy some
> groceries, then goes upstairs.

Once there, he places his New York *Times* on the pile.
Later he uses one or two days' numbers to wrap his gar-
bage in. Having finished his dinner, he turns on the TV,
and if at the office "someone should mention something
that is in the news, he will give a dry, sardonic answer
based upon the information he has garnered from TV."
He has gotten away with this for some time, although he is
terrified that he will be exposed. One of his recurring
nightmares, he tells Kozol, is that sometime someone will
hold out to him a page with writing on it and ask impa-
tiently, *"What does this mean?"* Confronted with this image
of his ultimate humiliation, he wakes from his nightmare
screaming.

The 60 million illiterates clearly include many such
professional people, always terrified of exposure, maintaining a precarious hold on the world assumed and mas-
tered by the educated. And if like that man 60 million are
functionally illiterate, another 60 million read at what is
charitably described as "the fifth-grade level." The number who read as many as *one* book a year, with "book"
defined so generously as to include a quasi-porno romance
and a How-to-Seem-Better-Than-You-Are manual, is 6
percent of the adult population. One "book" a year. The
other 94 percent depend for their awareness of actuality
entirely on TV, radio, hearsay, newspapers aimed at the
eight-year-old mind, and magazines devoted largely to
raising their readers' "self-esteem."

Consequently, compared with its industrialized peers,
the United States is defective in many other ways. Obvious
is its inferiority to Japan in industrial design. There, as
critic Douglas Davis writes, "We are several decades be-

hind our competitors," a fact muted and soft-focused by our accustomed habits of self-esteem. "But the cruel truth," notes Davis, "is that American consumer products, with few exceptions, are bland in style, deficient in flair and crude in workmanship." Likewise, America's inferiority to most European countries in social welfare is clear to anyone who travels with eyes open. Our rates of murder and violent crime dramatically surpass those elsewhere. And with twice Japan's rate of infant mortality, the United States has very little occasion for self-congratulation. In fact, among "civilized" countries, the United States ranks twenty-second in infant mortality, well behind France, Italy, what used to be the two Germanys, Austria, Belgium, and Britain. Even Spain and Ireland are our superiors there. Moreover, once someone gets born here, he or she is not out of trouble. More than three-quarters of the deaths of young people in America are violent, caused by suicide, murder, or accident—a world record. The *New York Times* announced in March 1990, "Children in the United States are more likely than children in eleven other industrialized countries to live in poverty, to live with only one parent or to be killed before they reach the age of twenty-five." Many are burned to death, the United States having the worst fire-safety record of all large industrial countries. Not to mention the dramatic figures on drug addiction.

Put the American predilection for violence and our romantic-sick love of firearms together with the American hunger for drugs and you get findings like this (*New York Times,* June 27, 1990):

U.S. IS BY FAR THE HOMICIDE CAPITAL OF THE INDUSTRIALIZED NATIONS

The homicide rate [i.e., murder rate: see *BAD Language*] among young men in the United States is 4 to 73 times the rate in other industrialized nations, Fed-

eral researchers have reported. They said firearms
were used in three-fourths of the killings in this country and in only one-fourth of those overseas.

In the land of the free virtually anyone is free to wield a
gun, and in the home of the brave, you are not considered
thoroughly brave if you back out of a quarrel even when a
gun has been produced.

In addition, the stupidity and ignorance of Americans
has long been a topic of hilarity in Europe. Instead of the
Greening of America, we can now speak of the Dumbing
of America—or, as Christopher Lasch has put it, the
Spread of Stupefaction. It is hardly news anymore that the
schools have failed to produce even a half-educated population. Only 42 percent of the seventeen-year-old students in American high schools can understand a
newspaper editorial, even in our dumbest papers—
although the cause may not be so much failure of "comprehension" as a cleverly concealed inability to read at all.
The scandal of slipping scores on the Scholastic Aptitude
Test has been apparent for years: between 1969 and 1989
the scores of high school seniors aiming at "college" fell 53
points. At most American universities, the majority of students spend the first year, and sometimes the second as
well, in "studies" that can only be termed remedial. Recently the New York Telephone Company had to test
57,000 people to find 2,100 bright enough to become operators or repairer-installers. And it's now no surprise to
hear a partner in a law firm complain that the products of
even the best law schools he interviews can't speak or write
articulately, let alone eloquently—these are young people
unable in today's TV and visual atmosphere to perceive
that the law is about little more than language precisely
construed and effectively deployed.

Schoolteachers must come from somewhere, and

many of them come from the intellectually incompetent classes. One public school teacher testifies: "A second-grade teacher in my school came up to me and asked me how many weeks in a year. . . . Then she asked me how many days in a year." Asked how she managed to know such things, the learned teacher answered that she'd learned in elementary school. Clearly, the curriculum, undemanding as it must necessarily be lest everyone fail, is too hard for many teachers, who simply avoid the bulk of things they don't understand. And speaking of academic matters, even if E. D. Hirsch may go too far in assuming the necessity of a standard set of things one must know for "cultural literacy," every day offers new and striking examples of public ignorance. One national newspaper recently printed a picture of President Bush receiving an honorary degree, taken at the moment the hood was slipped over his head. "President Bush," read the caption, "is presented his doctor of letters *sash*." This newspaper has won numerous Pulitzer prizes.

This progressive dumbing of America is visible in some unexpected places. Anyone who has been writing bank checks for fifty years will have noticed dumbing even there. Now, it's been felt necessary to provide on the check a little box within which you write the amount in figures, which seems to assume that otherwise you'd be at a loss where to put it. And on the back of checks there's a significant innovation, a precise place indicated where you are to write your endorsement, as if you didn't know which end of the check to sign. It is now necessary to inform Americans about to mail an envelope that "the Post Office will not deliver mail without proper postage," a point that formerly went without saying.

And how about the "Spell-Right" typewriter, popular because so few "writers" command their own language well enough to spell without mechanical assistance? How about a country where people are so stupid that they see nothing ridiculous about the idea of "rebates" when they spend a lot of money on something, instead of expecting that the price be lowered in the first place? Imagine solemnly handing over money, and then waiting until some is portentously handed back, and then feeling that you've been the beneficiary in a bargain transaction. And how about the new practice of scrutinizing the tickets of Amtrak passengers before they're allowed on the departure platform? The assumption is clearly that the illiterates (on an average day probably about 30 percent of one's fellows) can't read the ticket or the sign at the gate indicating the destination. And what are we to think of a culture in which the weather, not just locally but, God save the mark, all over the country, is deemed an interesting topic for TV news, to be solemnly commented on by costly personalities?

How about a country which spends billions of dollars on "exploring" outer space when millions of the poor and hungry sleep, like the natives of Calcutta, on its city streets? How about a nation in which tens of millions are so culturally and spiritually empty that their main way of defining themselves and achieving self-respect is to "go shopping"? What about a country slavering to Americanize Eastern Europe, nurturing there the values that bring us white stretch limos, Donald Trump, Jim and Tammy Bakker, Leona Helmsley, and Messrs. Milken and Boesky?

What about a country that declares its values and worth by electing as its President, and then reelecting, a superannuated movie star so ignorant of modern and contemporary history as to constitute a long-running comedy among the intelligent, a person so inattentive to world reality as to assert in the late 1980s that very few living Germans even remember the Second World War? Whose body of ideas embraced primarily the notion that school prayer and the abolition of taxes on the rich are what the country needs, together with the conviction that indigence and homelessness are voluntary?

When did the dumbing of America begin? Certainly not with, say Franklin and Jefferson. Some rude skeptics and vulgar wits, to whom nothing is sacred, might want to locate the origins of "creeping nincompoopism" (as one editorialist has called it) in the 1830s, when Joseph Smith took from dictation a number of miserably written narratives and injunctions conveyed to him by the angel Moroni and then persuaded a number of hicks to begin a new religion. Mark Twain thought the dumbing well advanced by his day, and some will say it reached something like the climax so far in 1978 with the mass suicides at Jonestown. By now the whole movement is clear enough to suggest two contemporary attendant phenomena, if not causes.

First, television, with its laugh tracks to inform the audience when it should laugh (in case the mugging and overstatement don't do the job), and its need to address its ads to the most ignorant, credulous, and psychologically insecure. Skepticism and criticism are rigorously repelled by it, for if they had a look-in, it could not serve as so satisfactory a mechanism of dumbing. And a second cause is the collapse of the public secondary school. When was a truant officer last seen?

There seems wide agreement that these two things are main causes of our intellectual and cultural predicament. Barbara Ehrenreich simply sums up the findings of "dozens of commentators" in noting that "American culture has been privatized, atomized, and perhaps irreversibly idiotized by the combination of television and Epcot-style education." Even admitting some disagreement about the precise reasons, one thing is clear: a minor cost of the dumbing is the transfer of American economic power to Japan. A major cost is the wiping-out of the amenity and nuance and complexity and charm that make a country worth living in.

And what's made it worse is the recent rapid complication of technology. The current United States can be defined as an immense accumulation of not terribly acute or attentive people obliged to operate a uniquely complex technology, which, all other things being equal, always wins. No wonder error and embarrassment lurk everywhere, and no wonder cover-up and bragging (that is, BAD) have become the favored national style. A standard sight today is an anxious young person requiring five minutes to complete a simple retail transaction, the time it takes to meet the demands of the monstrous buzzing, whistling, and humming machine which is at once cash register, current inventory establisher, issuer of receipts, and preventer of employee theft (and self-respect). Every employee a machine's toad. The puzzled and demeaned young clerk is a simpler version of the airline pilot confronted with ever-increasing dials and lights—which often don't work at all or which the pilot secretly disconnects to keep his job from becoming so complicated that he can't do it.

The natural result of all this is overcompensation, resulting most often in some form of BAD. Actual American life as experienced by most people is so boring, uniform, and devoid of significant soul, so isolated from traditions of the past and the resonances of European culture, that it demands to be "raised" and misrepresented as something wonderful. BAD thus becomes an understandable reaction to the national emptiness and dullness, and in its way it does represent a quest for at least the illusion of distinction and value. For example: if a town has no restaurant worth entering, it is some local comfort to cooperate with the restaurateur in the BAD game—taking seriously the pompous, illiterate menu, the fraudulent French, the balletic wine service, all the clumsy imitations of the real thing.

Because to have BAD you have to have two players, a presenter and a client, both engaged in a conspiracy against actuality. Again: if a town has no beauty, distinction, or charm, and is really populated only by money-grubbers, philistines, and self-satisfied provincials, it is a comfort to cooperate with the pretensions of the local "art gallery"-cum-gift shop and to acquire its hideous mass-produced sub-sculptures as if they were "works of art."

It is perhaps not necessary here to make the point that not everything in America is bad or BAD. Some taste survives here, enough to keep Muhammad Ali generally out of sight and not require him to speak in public, enough to recognize, if only implicitly and by silence, that the Vietnam War was a scandal. Some things, indeed, range from good to VERY GOOD, like the American open borders, when they've not been compromised by follies like the McCarran-Walter Act, and the American assumption that its citizens are free, and indeed are practically invited, to travel the world. Add the First Amendment, and you have a package of values so admirable as to be almost worth dying for. Diplomat and scholar George F. Kennan knows this, despite the bad press he gave America in his recent book *Sketches from a Life,* in which he confessed that a word like *bleak* would best describe his own country as he now sees it. He explains: "A reader might think that I saw in [the United States] only ugliness, vulgarity, and deterioration." But, he concludes, what has directed his vision to dwell on these blots is simple affection: "Had I not had my own sort of love of the place, these imperfections on its surface would not have hit me so hard. . . ." There is one day of the year when America should receive nothing but praise. That's July Fourth. On all other occasions, those who wish the United States well will vigorously distinguish the good from the bad, and especially from the BAD.

THE FUTURE OF **BAD**

The future of BAD is immense, to echo what Matthew Arnold said in 1879 about the future of poetry. He was wrong, of course, but not as wrong as we will be if we imagine that a little kicking ass and taking names is going to retard the progress of BAD. The new Goddess of Dullness is in the saddle, attended by her outriders Greed, Ignorance, and Publicity.

In short, BAD has gotten such a head start that nothing can slow it down much, even if we should blow up the teachers colleges; nationalize the airlines; make C, not B, the average grade again; reinstall Latin in the high schools; stop demeaning children by calling them kids and policemen by calling them cops; get rid of intercollegiate athletics; curb the national impulse to brag; raise the capital gains tax; teach a generation to sneer at advertising and to treat astrology with contempt; build bridges that don't collapse; stay out of space; persuade educated people that criticism is their main business; speak and write English and other languages with some taste and subtlety; get the homeless into a new Civilian Conservation Corps; produce intelligent movies; develop in the Navy higher standards of courage and discipline; start a few sophisticated national newspapers; give diners at BAD restaurants the guts to say, after the manager has asked them if they've enjoyed their dinner, "No"; abandon all remains of the self-congratulatory Cold War psychosis; improve the literacy of public signs and the taste of public sculpture; get people of artistic talent to design our stamps and coins; and develop public television into a medium free of all commerce. Because these things are not likely to happen, the only recourse is to laugh at BAD. If you don't, you're going to have to cry.

ABOUT THE AUTHOR

PAUL FUSSELL, essayist, literary critic, and cultural commentator, was born in California in 1924. Among his books are *The Great War and Modern Memory*, which won the National Book Award for Arts and Letters in 1976; *Abroad: British Literary Traveling Between the Wars; Class: A Guide Through the American Status System;* and *Wartime: Understanding and Behavior in the Second World War*. His essays, widely published in magazines in America and abroad, have been collected in *The Boy Scout Handbook and Other Observations* and *Thank God for the Atom Bomb and Other Essays*. He has taught English at Connecticut College and, for many years, at Rutgers, and he currently teaches at the University of Pennsylvania and lives in Philadelphia.